Standard Grade | Credit

Physics

Credit Level 2004

Credit Level 2005

Credit Level 2006

Credit Level 2007

Credit Level 2008

Leckie×Leckie

© Scottish Qualifications Authority

First exam published in 2004.
Published by Leckie & Leckie Ltd, 3rd Floor, 4 Queen Street, Edinburgh EH2 1JE
tel: 0131 220 6831 fax: 0131 225 9987 enquiries@leckieandleckie.co.uk www.leckieandleckie.co.uk

ISBN 978-1-84372-642-5

A CIP Catalogue record for this book is available from the British Library.

Leckie & Leckie is a division of Huveaux plc.

Leckie & Leckie is grateful to the copyright holders, as credited at the back of the book, for permission to use their material. Every effort has been made to trace the copyright holders and to obtain their permission for the use of copyright material. Leckie & Leckie will gladly receive information enabling them to rectify any error or omission in subsequent editions.

2004 | Credit

[BLANK PAGE]

FOR OFFICIAL USE

C

K & U	PS

Total Marks

3220/402

NATIONAL
QUALIFICATIONS
2004

FRIDAY, 28 MAY
10.50 AM – 12.35 PM

PHYSICS
STANDARD GRADE
Credit Level

Fill in these boxes and read what is printed below.

Full name of centre

Town

Forename(s)

Surname

Date of birth

Day Month Year   Scottish candidate number   Number of seat

1 All questions should be answered.

2 The questions may be answered in any order but all answers must be written clearly and legibly in this book.

3 Write your answer where indicated by the question or in the space provided after the question.

4 If you change your mind about your answer you may score it out and rewrite it in the space provided at the end of the answer book.

5 Before leaving the examination room you must give this book to the invigilator. If you do not, you may lose all the marks for this paper.

6 Any necessary data will be found in the **data sheet** on page two.

7 Care should be taken to give an appropriate number of significant figures in the final answers to questions.

SCOTTISH
QUALIFICATIONS
AUTHORITY

DATA SHEET

Speed of light in materials

Material	Speed in m/s
Air	$3{\cdot}0 \times 10^8$
Carbon dioxide	$3{\cdot}0 \times 10^8$
Diamond	$1{\cdot}2 \times 10^8$
Glass	$2{\cdot}0 \times 10^8$
Glycerol	$2{\cdot}1 \times 10^8$
Water	$2{\cdot}3 \times 10^8$

Speed of sound in materials

Material	Speed in m/s
Aluminium	5200
Air	340
Bone	4100
Carbon dioxide	270
Glycerol	1900
Muscle	1600
Steel	5200
Tissue	1500
Water	1500

Gravitational field strengths

	Gravitational field strength on the surface in N/kg
Earth	10
Jupiter	26
Mars	4
Mercury	4
Moon	1·6
Neptune	12
Saturn	11
Sun	270
Venus	9

Specific heat capacity of materials

Material	Specific heat capacity in J/kg °C
Alcohol	2350
Aluminium	902
Copper	386
Diamond	530
Glass	500
Glycerol	2400
Ice	2100
Lead	128
Water	4180

Specific latent heat of fusion of materials

Material	Specific latent heat of fusion in J/kg
Alcohol	$0{\cdot}99 \times 10^5$
Aluminium	$3{\cdot}95 \times 10^5$
Carbon dioxide	$1{\cdot}80 \times 10^5$
Copper	$2{\cdot}05 \times 10^5$
Glycerol	$1{\cdot}81 \times 10^5$
Lead	$0{\cdot}25 \times 10^5$
Water	$3{\cdot}34 \times 10^5$

Melting and boiling points of materials

Material	Melting point in °C	Boiling point in °C
Alcohol	−98	65
Aluminium	660	2470
Copper	1077	2567
Glycerol	18	290
Lead	328	1737
Turpentine	−10	156

Specific latent heat of vaporisation of materials

Material	Specific latent heat of vaporisation in J/kg
Alcohol	$11{\cdot}2 \times 10^5$
Carbon dioxide	$3{\cdot}77 \times 10^5$
Glycerol	$8{\cdot}30 \times 10^5$
Turpentine	$2{\cdot}90 \times 10^5$
Water	$22{\cdot}6 \times 10^5$

SI Prefixes and Multiplication Factors

Prefix	Symbol	Factor	
giga	G	1 000 000 000	$= 10^9$
mega	M	1 000 000	$= 10^6$
kilo	k	1000	$= 10^3$
milli	m	0·001	$= 10^{-3}$
micro	μ	0·000 001	$= 10^{-6}$
nano	n	0·000 000 001	$= 10^{-9}$

Marks | K&U | PS

1. A mobile phone can send signals on 3 different frequencies, 900 MHz, 1800 MHz and 1900 MHz.

(a) (i) Which signal has the longest wavelength?

.... 1

(ii) Calculate the wavelength of the 1800 MHz signal.

Space for working and answer

3

(b) At a base station, microwave signals from the mobile phone are converted into light signals for transmission along an optical fibre.

(i) State two advantages of sending light signals along an optical fibre compared to sending electrical signals along a wire.

....

.... 2

(ii) The time taken for light to travel along a glass optical fibre is 1·2 ms.

(A) State the speed at which signals travel along the optical fibre.

.... 1

(B) Calculate the length of the optical fibre.

Space for working and answer

2

Marks | K&U | PS

2. A colour television receiver displays 25 images on the screen every second.

(a) Calculate the number of images displayed on the screen in one minute.

> *Space for working and answer*

1

(b) The television receiver contains decoders.

State the function of a decoder.

....

.... 1

(c) In the colour television tube, three electron guns each send a beam of electrons to the screen.

(i) Why are **three** electron guns needed in a **colour** television tube?

....

.... 1

(ii) The diagram below shows the screen and the shadow mask in a colour television tube.

Use information from the diagram to explain why a shadow mask is needed.

....

....

.... 2

Marks | K&U | PS

3. A portable radio contains a rechargeable battery and a generator. The battery is charged by turning the handle of the generator.

(a) State the purpose of the battery.

.... 1

(b) The battery is fully discharged. The handle of the generator is turned 500 times by a constant force of 9·0 N. For each turn of the handle, the force moves through a distance of 400 mm.

(i) Show that the work done in charging the battery is 1800 J.

Space for working and answer

2

(ii) Only 90% of the work done in charging the battery is available as output energy from the battery.

(A) Calculate the output energy available.

Space for working and answer

2

(B) When operating, the radio takes a current of 250 mA. The voltage of the battery is 3 V.

Calculate the maximum time for which the radio operates.

Space for working and answer

2

Marks | K&U | PS

4. The circuit diagram of the wiring of a car's sidelights and headlights is shown.

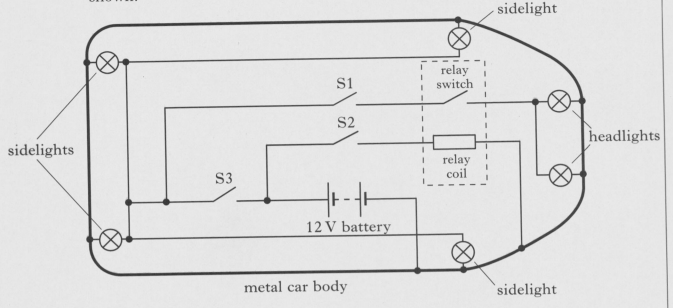

S1 is the headlight switch. S2 is the ignition switch.

When there is a current in the relay coil, the relay switch closes.

(a) Which lights are on when switch S3 **only** is closed?

.... 1

(b) At night the car has the sidelights on and the headlights on. The driver switches off the ignition. This opens the ignition switch.

Explain why **only** the headlights go out.

....

....

.... 2

Marks | K&U | PS

4. **(continued)**

(c) **Each** sidelight is rated at 12 V, 6 W, and **each** headlight is rated at 12 V, 55 W.

(i) Calculate the current in the battery when **only** the sidelights are on.

Space for working and answer

3

(ii) The driver leaves the car for 10 minutes with **only** the sidelights on.

Calculate the charge that flows through the battery in this time.

Space for working and answer

2

(iii) Each headlight gives out more light energy than each sidelight when on for the same time.

Explain why this happens.

....

....

....

2

[Turn over

Marks | K&U | PS

5. An entry system for a block of flats lets residents speak to callers before unlocking the outside door.

(a) A microphone at the outside door is connected through an amplifier to a loudspeaker in a flat.

microphone ⭘   amplifier   ◁ loudspeaker

The input power to the amplifier from the microphone is 5 mW and the output power from the amplifier is 2 W.

(i) Calculate the power gain of the amplifier.

Space for working and answer

2

(ii) The voltage across the loudspeaker is 4 V.

Calculate the resistance (impedance) of the loudspeaker.

Space for working and answer

2

5. (continued)

(*b*) The entry system allows a resident to unlock the outside door from the flat. The diagram below shows this part of this system.

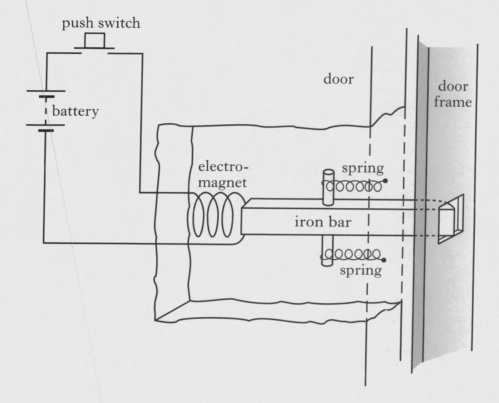

Explain how this part of the system operates to unlock the door.

....

....

....

....   2

[Turn over

Marks | K&U | PS

6. A person visits an optician for an eye test and is found to be long sighted in both eyes. The optician issues the following prescription for lenses.

	Power of lens required (D)
Left eye	+2·5
Right eye	+1·0

(a) State what is meant by long sight.

....

....   **1**

(b) Draw the shape of the lenses used to correct the defect in each eye.
Your drawings must show how the two lenses are different.

Shape of lens for left eye	
Shape of lens for right eye	

3

(c) Calculate the focal length of the lens prescribed for the left eye.

Space for working and answer

2

Marks | K&U | PS

7. A smoke detector contains two metal electrodes, a battery and an alarm circuit. Alpha radiation from a radioactive source ionises air between the two electrodes.

A voltage is applied across the electrodes. Although there is a gap between the two electrodes, there is a current between the electrodes. When there are smoke particles between the electrodes, this current is reduced. This sets off the alarm.

(a) (i) What is meant by ionisation?

....

....   1

   (ii) Explain how the current is produced in the gap between the electrodes.

....

....   1

(b) Apart from safety reasons, why is a source that emits alpha radiation more suitable in a smoke detector than a source that emits gamma radiation?

....

....   1

(c) State the unit of activity of a radioactive source.

....   1

Page eleven   **[Turn over**

Marks | K&U | PS

8. At a bottling plant, shampoo bottles on a conveyor pass a liquid level detector. Bottles filled to an acceptable level continue along the conveyor for packing. Bottles that are overfilled or underfilled are rejected.

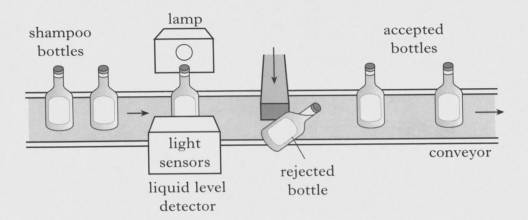

The liquid level detector consists of a lamp and two identical light sensors. The sensors are placed as shown in the diagram below. Light from the lamp can reach a sensor only when there is no shampoo between the lamp and the sensor.

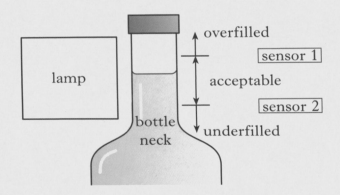

Part of the logic circuit of the liquid level detector is shown below.

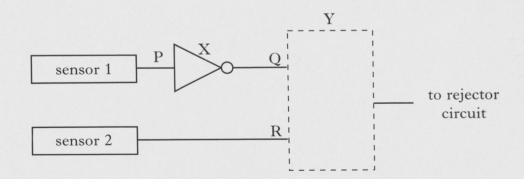

Page twelve

8. (continued)

The logic level outputs of a light sensor are as shown.

Light level at sensor	Logic level output
dark	0
light	1

(a) Name gate X.

....

1

(b) Complete the table to show the logic levels at P, Q and R when bottles filled to different levels are at the detector.

Liquid level	P	Q	R
Overfilled			
Acceptable			
Underfilled			

3

(c) The rejector circuit requires a logic level 1 to operate.

What type of gate at Y gives a logic 1 output only when a bottle is not filled to an acceptable level?

....

1

[Turn over

Marks | K&U | PS

9. Land speed records are calculated by timing a vehicle as it travels a measured distance of 2·0 km.

(a) Explain whether the average speed or the instantaneous speed of the vehicle can be calculated from these measurements.

....

....

....   2

(b) A vehicle travels the measured distance at a constant speed of 220 m/s. Calculate the time taken.

Space for working and answer

2

(c) At the end of the measured distance, the driver switches off the engine and opens a parachute to brake.

The speed-time graph shows the motion of the vehicle from this time.

The mass of the vehicle is 3000 kg.

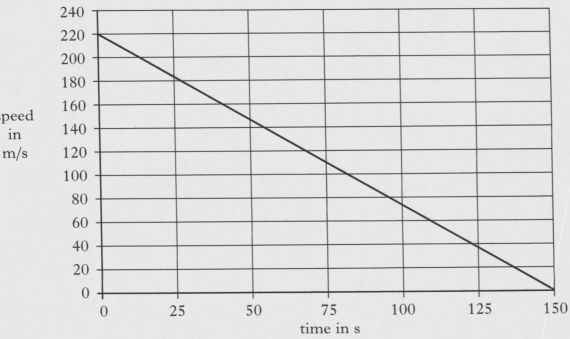

Marks | K&U | PS

9. *(c)* **(continued)**

(i) Explain how the parachute helps to reduce the speed of the vehicle.

....

.... **1**

(ii) Calculate the distance travelled by the vehicle from the time the parachute opens until the vehicle stops.

> *Space for working and answer*

2

(iii) Calculate the acceleration of the vehicle while it is slowing down.

> *Space for working and answer*

2

(iv) Calculate the unbalanced force on the vehicle while it is slowing down.

> *Space for working and answer*

2

[Turn over

Marks | K&U | PS

9. (c) (continued)

(v) Calculate the kinetic energy of the vehicle at the instant the parachute opens.

Space for working and answer

2

10. A metal guitar string, fixed to a wooden base, is connected to an oscilloscope. A magnet is placed so that the string is between the poles of the magnet, as shown.

When the string is plucked, a sound is produced and a voltage is induced in the string. The induced voltage is displayed on the screen of the oscilloscope.

(a) (i) Why is a voltage induced when the string is plucked?

....

.... 1

(ii) State one change that can be made so that a larger voltage is induced.

.... 1

10. (continued)

(b) The oscilloscope gain setting and trace are shown.

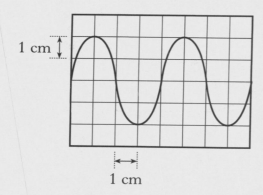

GAIN

Calculate the peak voltage.

Space for working and answer

2

(c) A different metal string is used to produce a louder sound of higher frequency. No other changes are made to the equipment.

Draw a possible new trace on the blank screen below.

trace produced
by original
string

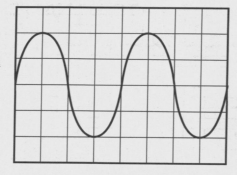

trace produced
by second
string

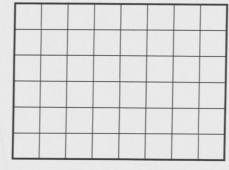

2

Marks | K&U | PS

11. A mass of 500 g of a substance is heated with a 30 W heater. A temperature probe is inserted into the substance.

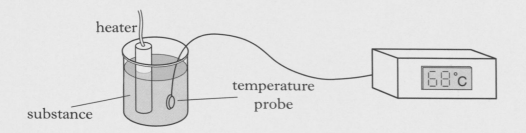

The substance is initially solid and at room temperature. The graph below shows the variation of the temperature of the substance from the time the heater is switched on.

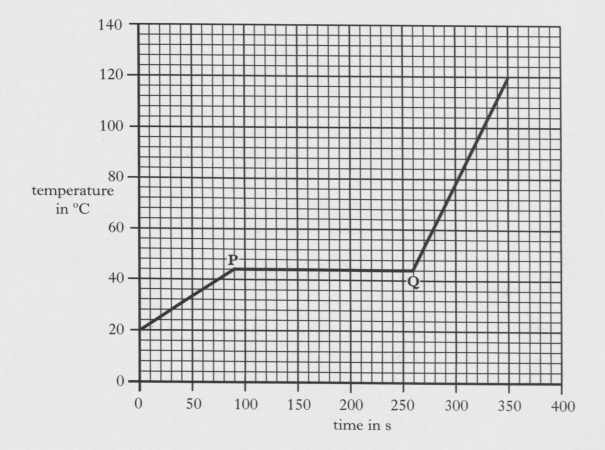

(a) State the value of room temperature.

.... 1

Marks | K&U | PS

11. (continued)

(b) (i) Why does the temperature of the substance remain constant between P and Q?

....

1

(ii) Calculate the energy transferred by the heater during the time interval PQ.

Space for working and answer

3

(iii) Calculate the specific latent heat of fusion of the substance.

Space for working and answer

2

[Turn over

Marks K&U PS

12. A bicycle lamp contains four LEDs W, X, Y and Z and a 3 V battery. The lamp uses a pulse generator to make two of the LEDs flash. A simplified circuit diagram of the bicycle lamp is shown.

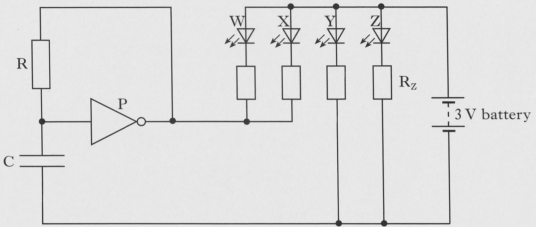

(a) (i) Which LEDs flash when the lamp is operating?

.... **1**

(ii) State two changes that could be made to the circuit to increase the frequency at which the LEDs flash.

....

.... **2**

(b) When LED Z is lit, the current in it is 15 mA and the voltage across it is 1·8 V.

Calculate the resistance of R_Z.

Space for working and answer

3

Marks | K&U | PS

13. The table below has information about three telescopes used to detect radiation from space.

objective lens	Refracting telescope in Edinburgh, with 150 mm diameter objective lens.
detector — curved reflector	Radio telescope at Jodrell Bank, with a curved reflector of diameter 76 m.
detector — curved reflector	Radio telescope at Arecibo, Puerto Rico, with a curved reflector of diameter 300 m.

(a) What type of radiation is detected by a refracting telescope?

.... 1

(b) Why are different types of telescope used to detect radiation from space?

....

.... 1

(c) In a radio telescope, where is the detector placed in relation to the curved reflector?

....

.... 1

(d) Explain which of the three telescopes shown above is best for detecting very weak radio signals from deep space.

....

....

....

.... 2

Marks | K&U | PS

14. A space vehicle consists of a rocket engine, fuel and a probe. When sitting on the launch pad, the total mass of the space vehicle is 150 000 kg.

(a) Calculate the weight of the space vehicle on the launch pad.

> *Space for working and answer*

2

(b) The space vehicle is launched. Shortly after lift-off, it is at a height of 650 km above the surface of the Earth. At this time, 80 000 kg of fuel have been used.

Give **two** reasons why the weight of the space vehicle is now less than it was on the launch pad.

Reason one..

....

Reason two ....

....

2

(c) The space vehicle travels into a region of space where the gravitational field strength is zero. The engine is now switched off.

Describe and explain the motion of the vehicle.

....

....

....

2

Marks | K&U | PS

15. Some members of the electromagnetic spectrum are named below.

TV and Radio		Infrared	Visible light		X-rays	Gamma rays

(a) Write the names of the missing radiations in the correct spaces in the diagram above.

2

(b) State **one** radiation that has a lower frequency than visible light.

....

1

(c) State **one** detector of X-rays.

....

1

(d) State **one** medical use of infrared radiation.

....

1

[END OF QUESTION PAPER]

YOU MAY USE THE SPACE ON THIS PAGE TO REWRITE ANY ANSWER YOU HAVE DECIDED TO CHANGE IN THE MAIN PART OF THE ANSWER BOOKLET. TAKE CARE TO WRITE IN CAREFULLY THE APPROPRIATE QUESTION NUMBER.

DO NOT WRITE IN THIS MARGIN

K&U	PS

[BLANK PAGE]

FOR OFFICIAL USE

C

K & U	PS

Total Marks

3220/402

NATIONAL
QUALIFICATIONS
2005

TUESDAY, 24 MAY
10.50 AM – 12.35 PM

PHYSICS
STANDARD GRADE
Credit Level

Fill in these boxes and read what is printed below.

Full name of centre

Town

Forename(s)

Surname

Date of birth
Day Month Year

Scottish candidate number

Number of seat

1 All questions should be answered.

2 The questions may be answered in any order but all answers must be written clearly and legibly in this book.

3 Write your answer where indicated by the question or in the space provided after the question.

4 If you change your mind about your answer you may score it out and rewrite it in the space provided at the end of the answer book.

5 Before leaving the examination room you must give this book to the invigilator. If you do not, you may lose all the marks for this paper.

6 Any necessary data will be found in the **data sheet** on page two.

7 Care should be taken to give an appropriate number of significant figures in the final answers to questions.

SCOTTISH
QUALIFICATIONS
AUTHORITY

DATA SHEET

Speed of light in materials

Material	Speed in m/s
Air	$3{\cdot}0 \times 10^8$
Carbon dioxide	$3{\cdot}0 \times 10^8$
Diamond	$1{\cdot}2 \times 10^8$
Glass	$2{\cdot}0 \times 10^8$
Glycerol	$2{\cdot}1 \times 10^8$
Water	$2{\cdot}3 \times 10^8$

Speed of sound in materials

Material	Speed in m/s
Aluminium	5200
Air	340
Bone	4100
Carbon dioxide	270
Glycerol	1900
Muscle	1600
Steel	5200
Tissue	1500
Water	1500

Gravitational field strengths

	Gravitational field strength on the surface in N/kg
Earth	10
Jupiter	26
Mars	4
Mercury	4
Moon	1·6
Neptune	12
Saturn	11
Sun	270
Venus	9

Specific heat capacity of materials

Material	Specific heat capacity in J/kg °C
Alcohol	2350
Aluminium	902
Copper	386
Diamond	530
Glass	500
Glycerol	2400
Ice	2100
Lead	128
Water	4180

Specific latent heat of fusion of materials

Material	Specific latent heat of fusion in J/kg
Alcohol	$0{\cdot}99 \times 10^5$
Aluminium	$3{\cdot}95 \times 10^5$
Carbon dioxide	$1{\cdot}80 \times 10^5$
Copper	$2{\cdot}05 \times 10^5$
Glycerol	$1{\cdot}81 \times 10^5$
Lead	$0{\cdot}25 \times 10^5$
Water	$3{\cdot}34 \times 10^5$

Melting and boiling points of materials

Material	Melting point in °C	Boiling point in °C
Alcohol	−98	65
Aluminium	660	2470
Copper	1077	2567
Glycerol	18	290
Lead	328	1737
Turpentine	−10	156

Specific latent heat of vaporisation of materials

Material	Specific latent heat of vaporisation in J/kg
Alcohol	$11{\cdot}2 \times 10^5$
Carbon dioxide	$3{\cdot}77 \times 10^5$
Glycerol	$8{\cdot}30 \times 10^5$
Turpentine	$2{\cdot}90 \times 10^5$
Water	$22{\cdot}6 \times 10^5$

SI Prefixes and Multiplication Factors

Prefix	Symbol	Factor	
giga	G	1 000 000 000	$= 10^9$
mega	M	1 000 000	$= 10^6$
kilo	k	1000	$= 10^3$
milli	m	0·001	$= 10^{-3}$
micro	μ	0·000 001	$= 10^{-6}$
nano	n	0·000 000 001	$= 10^{-9}$

1. A car driver listens to a radio station broadcasting on 1500 kHz.

(a) Calculate the wavelength of the radio broadcast.

Space for working and answer

2

(b) The table shows the frequency range of the different wavebands on the radio receiver.

Waveband	Frequency range
long wave	30 kHz – 300 kHz
medium wave	300 kHz – 3 MHz
short wave	3 MHz – 30 MHz
F.M.	30 MHz – 300 MHz

From the table, write down the waveband of the radio station that the driver is listening to.

....

1

(c) A passenger in the car listens to a personal CD player.
The car enters a tunnel.

radio transmitter

As the car enters the tunnel, the sound from the radio fades, but the sound from the CD player can still be heard.

(i) Explain why the sound from the radio fades.

....

....

1

(ii) Explain why the sound from the CD player can still be heard.

....

....

1

Marks | K&U | PS

2. A television receiver is used to pick up a signal from a television transmitter.

(a) The block diagram represents a television receiver.

```
[aerial] → [        ] →  [audio      ] → [audio     ] → [loudspeaker]
                          [decoder    ]   [amplifier ]

                      →  [video      ] → [video     ] → [picture tube]
                          [decoder    ]   [amplifier ]
```

(i) On the diagram, label the part of the receiver that has been left blank.   1

(ii) State the purpose of the aerial.

....

....   1

(iii) One other necessary part of the television receiver is not shown on the block diagram.

Name this part.

....   1

(iv) Which part of the television receiver transforms electrical energy to light energy?

....   1

(b) In the transmitter, a video signal is combined with a carrier wave to produce a signal for transmission.

(i) Circle the correct phrase to complete this sentence.

The carrier wave has a frequency that is $\left\{ \begin{array}{l} \text{higher than} \\ \text{the same as} \\ \text{lower than} \end{array} \right\}$ the

frequency of the video signal.   1

(ii) Why is the carrier wave needed for transmission?

....

....   1

(iii) Name the process of combining the waves for transmission.

....   1

3. A student sets up the apparatus **exactly** as shown to measure the speed of sound in air.

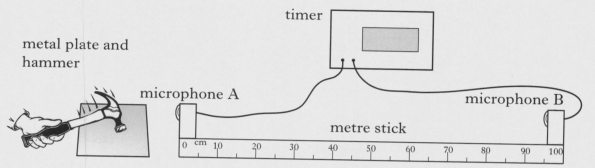

Striking the metal plate with the hammer produces a sound. Timing starts when the sound reaches microphone A, and stops when the same sound reaches microphone B.

(*a*) The student carries out the experiment three times and records the results shown in the table.

trial	distance between microphones (m)	time recorded on timer (s)
1	1·00	0·00287
2	1·00	0·00282
3	1·00	0·00286

Use **all** of the student's results to calculate the value of the speed of sound.

Space for working and answer

3

(*b*) Suggest a reason why the student's results do **not** give the value of 340 m/s for the speed of sound in air, as quoted in the data sheet.

....

....

1

Marks | K&U | PS

4. A mains vacuum cleaner contains a motor that takes 3·0 s to reach full speed after being switched on. The graph shows how the current in the motor varies from the time the motor is switched on.

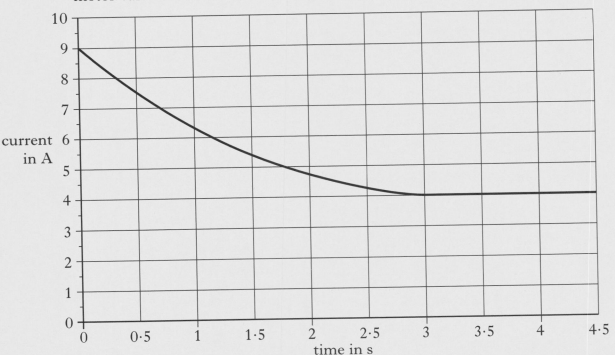

(*a*) (i) State the current when the motor has reached full speed.

.... **1**

(ii) Calculate the power of the motor when it has reached full speed.

Space for working and answer

3

(*b*) The vacuum cleaner is connected to the mains supply by a flex fitted with a fused plug.

(i) All the fuses shown are available.

3 ampere		5 ampere
10 ampere		13 ampere

Which one of these fuses is **most** suitable for fitting in the plug?

.... **1**

Marks   K&U   PS

4. (*b*) **(continued)**

    (ii)   State the purpose of the fuse fitted in the plug.

    ....

    ....   **1**

    (iii)   Explain why the fuse must be connected in the live wire.

    ....

    ....

    ....   **1**

[Turn over

Marks K&U PS

5. A post office contains an emergency alarm circuit. Each of three cashiers has an alarm switch fitted as shown. Lamps come on and a bell sounds if an alarm switch is closed.

Switch
P

Switch
Q

Switch
R

The circuit diagram for the alarm is shown.

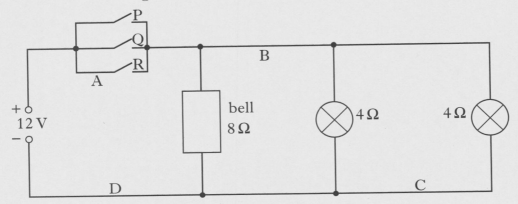

(a) The alarm circuit is to be controlled by a master switch.

Which position, A, B, C or D, is most suitable for the master switch?

1

(b) Each lamp has a resistance of 4 Ω and the bell has a resistance of 8 Ω. The circuit uses a 12 V supply.

(i) Calculate the total resistance of the alarm circuit.

Space for working and answer

2

DO NOT WRITE IN THIS MARGIN

Marks | K&U | PS

5. (*b*) **(continued)**

(ii) Calculate the current from the supply when the alarm is operating.

Space for working and answer

2

(*c*) Brighter lamps are fitted in the alarm circuit.

Explain how this change affects the resistance of the circuit.

....

....

.... **2**

[Turn over

DO NOT WRITE IN THIS MARGIN

Marks	K&U	PS

6. In the eye, refraction of light occurs at the cornea and at the eye lens.

(*a*) What is meant by refraction of light?

....

.... **1**

(*b*) The diagram below shows light rays entering the eye of a short-sighted person.

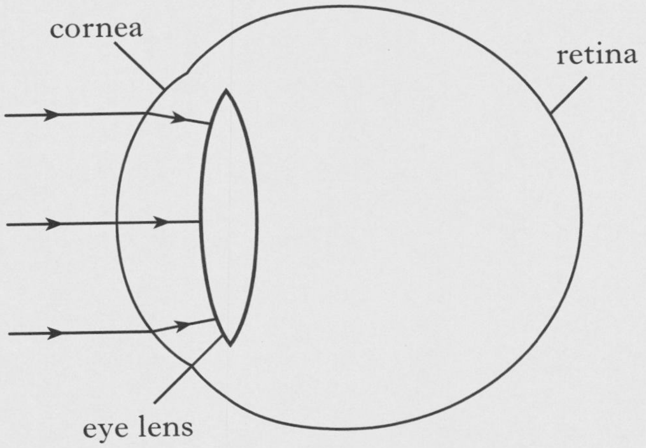

(i) Complete the diagram above to show how the light rays reach the retina of this short-sighted eye. **1**

(ii) A concave lens of focal length 400 mm is needed to correct the vision in this eye.

Calculate the power of this lens.

Space for working and answer **2**

Marks | K&U | PS

6. (continued)

(c) Short-sight can be corrected using a laser to reshape the cornea.

(i) For this treatment a pulsed laser is used. Each pulse lasts for a time of $0 \cdot 2 \, ms$ and transfers $5 \, mJ$ of energy.

Calculate the power rating of the laser.

Space for working and answer

2

(ii) What effect does laser surgery have on the focal length of the cornea?

.... **1**

(iii) When a laser is in use, a warning sign similar to the one shown must be displayed.

Why must a warning sign be displayed?

....

.... **1**

[Turn over

Marks | K&U | PS

7. Radioactive sources are used in medical investigations.

(*a*) A technician uses a Geiger-Muller tube, a counter and a timer to measure the half-life of a radioactive source. The source and the tube are placed in a lead box to exclude background radiation.

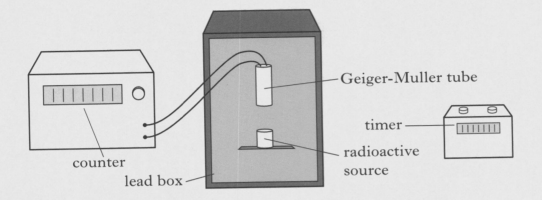

Geiger-Muller tube

timer

counter

radioactive source

lead box

(i) Describe how the apparatus is used to measure the half-life of the radioactive source.

....

....

....

....

....

....

3

(ii) The half-life of the source is 10 minutes. The initial count rate is 1200 counts per minute.

Calculate the count rate after 40 minutes.

Space for working and answer

2

7. (continued)

   (*b*) Dose equivalent measures the biological effect of radiation.

      (i) What unit is used to measure dose equivalent?

          ....   **1**

      (ii) State **two** factors that dose equivalent depends on.

          ....

          ....   **2**

[Turn over

Marks | K&U | PS

8. The circuit shown is used to investigate the switching action of a transistor.

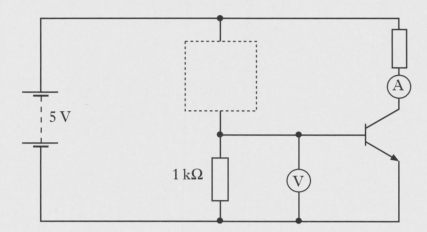

(a) Draw the symbol for a variable resistor in the dotted box in the above diagram.

1

(b) The graph shows how the ammeter reading varies with the voltmeter reading when the resistance of the variable resistor is changed.

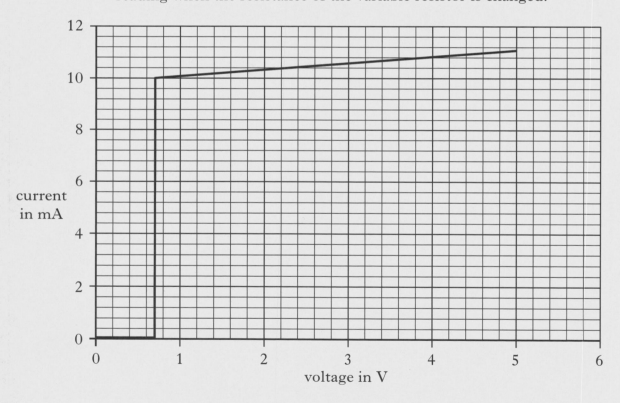

(i) State the voltage at which the transistor starts to conduct.

.... 1

DO NOT WRITE IN THIS MARGIN

Marks | K&U | PS

8. **(*b*) (continued)**

(ii) Calculate the voltage across the variable resistor when the transistor starts to conduct.

Space for working and answer

1

(iii) Calculate the resistance of the variable resistor when the transistor starts to conduct.

Space for working and answer

2

[Turn over

Marks | K&U | PS

9. A machine packs eggs into boxes. The eggs travel along a conveyor belt and pass through a light gate that operates a counter. After the correct number of eggs has passed through the light gate, the counter resets and the box is exchanged for an empty one.

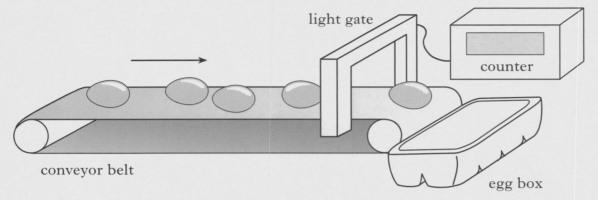

(a) The light gate consists of a light source and detector.

State a suitable component to be used as the detector.

.... 1

(b) Part of the counter circuit is shown.

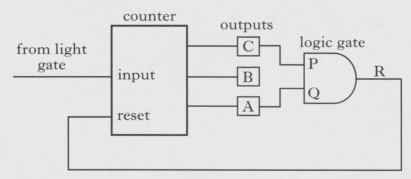

The input to the counter goes to logic 1 every time an egg passes through the light gate. When the reset to the counter goes to logic 1, the outputs go to zero.

The table below shows the logic states of the three outputs A, B and C of the counter as eggs pass the detector.

Number of eggs	A	B	C
0	0	0	0
1	0	0	1
2	0	1	0
3	0	1	1
4	1	0	0
5	1	0	1
6	1	1	0
7	1	1	1

Marks | K&U | PS

9. *(b)* **(continued)**

(i) Complete the truth table for the logic gate shown.

P	Q	R
0	0	
0	1	
1	0	
1	1	

1

(ii) How many eggs are being packed into each box when the logic gate is connected to the counter outputs as shown?

....

1

(iii) Complete the diagram below to show how the logic gate should be connected to the counter outputs so that six eggs can be packed in a box.

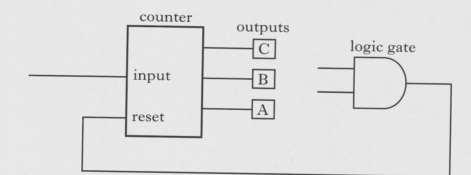

1

[Turn over

Marks | K&U | PS

10. A bobsleigh team competes in a race.

(a) Starting from rest, the bobsleigh reaches a speed of 11 m/s after a time of 3·2 s.

Calculate the acceleration of the bobsleigh.

Space for working and answer

2

(b) The bobsleigh completes the 1200 m race in a time of 42·0 s.

Calculate the average speed of the bobsleigh.

Space for working and answer

2

(c) Describe how the instantaneous speed of the bobsleigh could be measured as it crosses the finish line.

....

....

....

....

....

2

Marks | K&U | PS

10. (continued)

(*d*) To travel as quickly as possible, frictional forces must be minimised. State **two** methods of reducing friction.

....

.... **2**

[Turn over

Marks | K&U | PS

11. A train travels up a mountain carrying skiers in winter and tourists in summer.

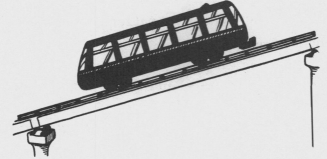

(*a*) The graph shows how the speed of the train varies with time for the journey in winter.

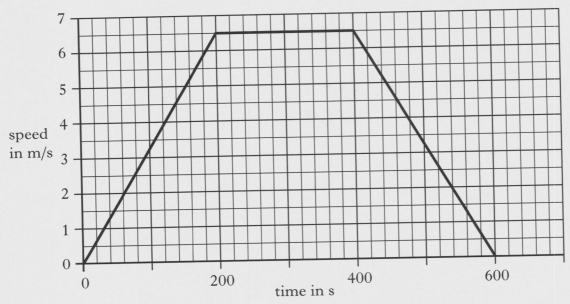

(i) Calculate the acceleration of the train during the first 200 s.

Space for working and answer

2

(ii) Calculate the length of the journey.

Space for working and answer

2

11. (continued)

(*b*) The mass of the train is 15 000 kg. During the journey the train travels through a height of 460 m.

Calculate the potential energy gained by the train.

> *Space for working and answer*

2

(*c*) In summer, the train takes a time of 1200 s to travel up the mountain so that tourists can enjoy the view. The acceleration and deceleration of the train remain the same as in winter. The graph below again shows the motion of the train in winter.

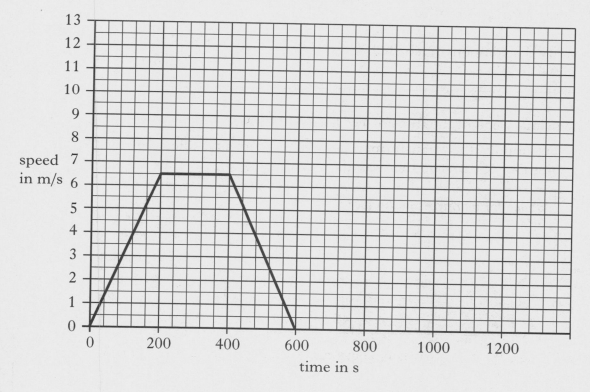

Using the axes given above, sketch a second graph showing the motion of the train in summer.
(Calculations are not required.)

2

[Turn over

Marks | K&U | PS

12. An electric toothbrush contains a rechargeable battery. The battery is recharged using a transformer connected to a 230 V a.c. supply. The primary coil and the core of the transformer are sealed into the base unit. The 5 V secondary coil of the transformer is part of the toothbrush.

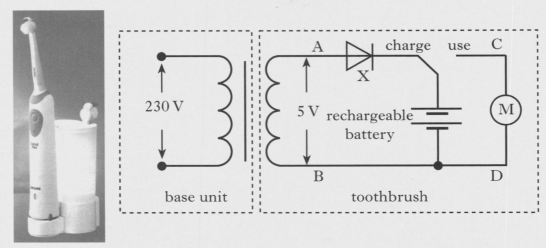

To charge the battery, the toothbrush is placed on the base unit, with the switch in the "charge" position.

(a) Identify the component labelled X.

....

1

(b) The primary coil of the transformer has 6440 turns.

(i) Assuming the transformer is 100% efficient, calculate the number of turns on the secondary coil.

Space for working and answer

2

(ii) When the toothbrush is charging, the current in the secondary coil is 50 mA.

(A) Calculate the output power of the transformer.

Space for working and answer

2

Marks | K&U | PS

12. **(*b*)(ii)** **(continued)**

(B) In practice, the transformer is only 40% efficient.

Calculate the current in the primary coil.

Space for working and answer

3

(iii) State **one** reason why a transformer is less than 100% efficient.

....

1

(*c*) Sketch the trace seen when an oscilloscope is connected across:

(i) AB when the battery is being charged;

(ii) CD when the toothbrush is removed from the base unit and the switch is in the "use" position.

Values need not be shown on either sketch.

AB

CD

2

[Turn over

Marks

13. The apparatus shown is used to calculate the value of the specific latent heat of vaporisation of water.

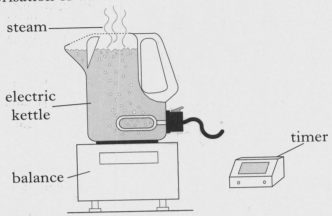

The electric kettle is rated at 3·0 kW. The kettle containing water is placed on the balance. The lid of the kettle is removed and the kettle is switched on. Once the water starts to boil, the kettle is left switched on for a further 85·0 s before being switched off.

(a) Calculate how much electrical energy is supplied to the kettle in 85·0 s.

Space for working and answer

2

(b) The reading on the balance decreases by 0·12 kg during the 85·0 s.

(i) Assuming all the electrical energy supplied is transferred to the water, calculate the value of the specific latent heat of vaporisation of water obtained in the experiment.

Space for working and answer

2

(ii) The accepted value for the specific latent heat of vaporisation of water is $22·6 \times 10^5$ J/kg.

Suggest why there is a difference between this value and the value obtained in (b)(i).

....

....

1

14. An astronomer uses a telescope and a camera to take a photograph of a distant galaxy.

camera   telescope   distant galaxy

(a) The table shows a number of lenses that are available for use in the telescope.

lens	type	focal length (mm)	diameter (mm)
P	concave	15	10
Q	convex	15	10
R	convex	1000	10
S	convex	1000	100
T	concave	1000	100

From the table, select the most suitable lenses for use as the eyepiece and the objective of the telescope.

Eyepiece [ ]   Objective [ ]

2

(b) The astronomer examines the photograph using a magnifying glass.

Complete the ray diagram to show how the magnifying glass can be used to form an image of the photograph.

Your diagram must show the position of the image.

photograph

focus   focus

3

Marks | K&U | PS

15. A spacecraft consisting of a rocket and a lunar probe is launched from the Earth to the Moon.

(*a*) At lift-off from the Earth, the spacecraft has a weight of 7100 kN. The thrust from the engines is 16 000 kN.

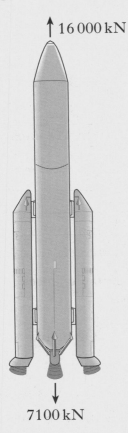

↑ 16 000 kN

↓

7100 kN

(i) Calculate the unbalanced force acting on the spacecraft.

> *Space for working and answer*

1

(ii) Calculate the mass of the spacecraft.

> *Space for working and answer*

1

15. (*a*) **(continued)**

(iii) Calculate the initial acceleration of the spacecraft.

Space for working and answer

2

(*b*) As it approaches the Moon, the probe is detached from the rocket and goes into lunar orbit.

(i) While orbiting the Moon, the probe takes images of the Moon's surface. This data is sent to Earth using radio waves. The distance between the probe and Earth is 384 000 km.

Calculate the time taken for the data to reach Earth.

Space for working and answer

2

(ii) The Moon is a natural satellite and the probe is an artificial satellite.

Explain what a satellite is.

....

....

1

(iii) The probe orbits the Moon because of the Moon's gravitational field.

Explain why the probe does not crash into the Moon.

....

....

....

1

[END OF QUESTION PAPER]

DO NOT
WRITE IN
THIS
MARGIN

K&U | PS

YOU MAY USE THE SPACE ON THIS PAGE TO REWRITE ANY ANSWER
YOU HAVE DECIDED TO CHANGE IN THE MAIN PART OF THE ANSWER
BOOKLET. TAKE CARE TO WRITE IN CAREFULLY THE APPROPRIATE
QUESTION NUMBER.

K&U | PS

[BLANK PAGE]

FOR OFFICIAL USE

C

K & U	PS

Total Marks

3220/402

NATIONAL
QUALIFICATIONS
2006

WEDNESDAY, 17 MAY
10.50 AM – 12.35 PM

PHYSICS
STANDARD GRADE
Credit Level

Fill in these boxes and read what is printed below.

Full name of centre

Town

Forename(s)

Surname

Date of birth
Day   Month   Year

Scottish candidate number

Number of seat

Reference may be made to the Physics Data Booklet.

1 All questions should be answered.

2 The questions may be answered in any order but all answers must be written clearly and legibly in this book.

3 Write your answer where indicated by the question or in the space provided after the question.

4 If you change your mind about your answer you may score it out and rewrite it in the space provided at the end of the answer book.

5 Before leaving the examination room you must give this book to the invigilator. If you do not, you may lose all the marks for this paper.

6 Any necessary data will be found in the **data sheet** on page two.

7 Care should be taken to give an appropriate number of significant figures in the final answers to questions.

SCOTTISH
QUALIFICATIONS
AUTHORITY

SA 3220/402 6/22770

©

DATA SHEET

Speed of light in materials

Material	Speed in m/s
Air	$3 \cdot 0 \times 10^8$
Carbon dioxide	$3 \cdot 0 \times 10^8$
Diamond	$1 \cdot 2 \times 10^8$
Glass	$2 \cdot 0 \times 10^8$
Glycerol	$2 \cdot 1 \times 10^8$
Water	$2 \cdot 3 \times 10^8$

Speed of sound in materials

Material	Speed in m/s
Aluminium	5200
Air	340
Bone	4100
Carbon dioxide	270
Glycerol	1900
Muscle	1600
Steel	5200
Tissue	1500
Water	1500

Gravitational field strengths

	Gravitational field strength on the surface in N/kg
Earth	10
Jupiter	26
Mars	4
Mercury	4
Moon	1·6
Neptune	12
Saturn	11
Sun	270
Venus	9

Specific heat capacity of materials

Material	Specific heat capacity in J/kg °C
Alcohol	2350
Aluminium	902
Copper	386
Diamond	530
Glass	500
Glycerol	2400
Ice	2100
Lead	128
Water	4180

Specific latent heat of fusion of materials

Material	Specific latent heat of fusion in J/kg
Alcohol	$0 \cdot 99 \times 10^5$
Aluminium	$3 \cdot 95 \times 10^5$
Carbon dioxide	$1 \cdot 80 \times 10^5$
Copper	$2 \cdot 05 \times 10^5$
Glycerol	$1 \cdot 81 \times 10^5$
Lead	$0 \cdot 25 \times 10^5$
Water	$3 \cdot 34 \times 10^5$

Melting and boiling points of materials

Material	Melting point in °C	Boiling point in °C
Alcohol	−98	65
Aluminium	660	2470
Copper	1077	2567
Glycerol	18	290
Lead	328	1737
Turpentine	−10	156

Specific latent heat of vaporisation of materials

Material	Specific latent heat of vaporisation in J/kg
Alcohol	$11 \cdot 2 \times 10^5$
Carbon dioxide	$3 \cdot 77 \times 10^5$
Glycerol	$8 \cdot 30 \times 10^5$
Turpentine	$2 \cdot 90 \times 10^5$
Water	$22 \cdot 6 \times 10^5$

SI Prefixes and Multiplication Factors

Prefix	Symbol	Factor	
giga	G	1 000 000 000	$= 10^9$
mega	M	1 000 000	$= 10^6$
kilo	k	1000	$= 10^3$
milli	m	0·001	$= 10^{-3}$
micro	μ	0·000 001	$= 10^{-6}$
nano	n	0·000 000 001	$= 10^{-9}$

DO NOT WRITE IN THIS MARGIN

1. A computer is connected to the Internet by means of a copper wire and a glass optical fibre as shown.

computer

copper wire

optical fibre junction

optical fibre

(a) In the table below, enter:

   (i) the speed of the signal in each material;

   (ii) the type of signal in each material.

	Copper wire	Glass optical fibre
Speed of signal		
Type of signal		

Marks: 2, 2

(b) Complete the diagram to show how the signal travels along the optical fibre.

optical fibre junction

optical fibre

Marks: 2

(c) Copper wire or glass optical fibre can be used in telecommunication systems.

   (i) Explain which material, copper or glass, would need less repeater amplifiers over a long distance.

....

....

Marks: 2

   (ii) A broadband communication system carries 100 television channels and 200 phone channels.

      Explain which material, copper or glass, should be used in this system.

....

....

Marks: 2

Marks | K&U | PS

2. A ship has a satellite navigation system. A receiver on the ship picks up signals from three global positioning satellites.

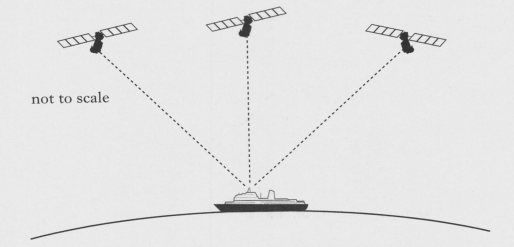

not to scale

These satellites can transmit radio signals at three different frequencies, 1176 MHz, 1228 MHz and 1575 MHz. The satellites orbit at a height of 20 200 km above the Earth's surface.

(a)   (i)   State the speed of the radio signals.

....

1

(ii)   One of the satellites is directly above the ship.

Calculate the time taken for the signal from this satellite to reach the ship.

Space for working and answer

2

(iii)   Calculate the wavelength of the 1228 MHz signal.

Space for working and answer

2

2. (continued)

(b) State which of the three signals has the shortest wavelength.

.... **1**

(c) One of the global positioning satellites is shown below.

curved reflector

transmitter

(i) Complete the diagram below to show the effect of the curved reflector on the transmitted signals.

2

(ii) A satellite in orbit a few hundred kilometres above Earth has a period of one hour. A geostationary satellite orbits 36 000 km above Earth.

Suggest the period of the global positioning satellite.

.... **1**

[Turn over

DO NOT
WRITE IN
THIS
MARGIN

Marks | K&U | PS

3. Two students are investigating voltage, current and resistance.

(*a*) The first student builds the circuit shown.

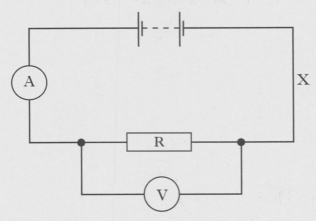

The ammeter displays a current of 0·10 A and the voltmeter displays a voltage of 3·0 V.

(i) Calculate the resistance of R when the current is 0·10 A.

Space for working and answer

2

(ii) The student inserts another ammeter at position X.

What is the reading on this ammeter?

.... 1

(*b*) The second student uses the **same** resistor in the circuit below.

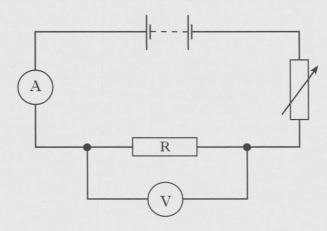

Marks | K&U | PS

3. **(b) (continued)**

This student obtains the following set of results.

Result number	Voltage across R (V)	Current through R (A)
1	6·0	0·20
2	7·5	0·25
3	9·0	0·30
4	10·0	0·35
5	12·0	0·40

(i) Describe how these different values of voltage and current are obtained.

....

.... **2**

(ii) Explain which result should be retaken.

....

.... **2**

(c) What additional information about resistance does the second student's experiment give compared to the first student's experiment?

....

....

.... **1**

[Turn over

Marks

4. A circuit breaker as shown below is used in a circuit.

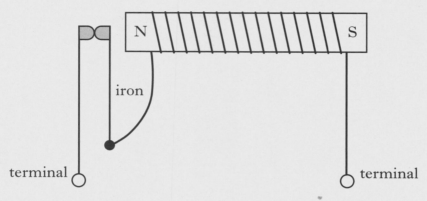

(a) (i) State **one** advantage of a circuit breaker compared to a fuse.

....

.... 1

(ii) The circuit breaker breaks the circuit when the current becomes too high.

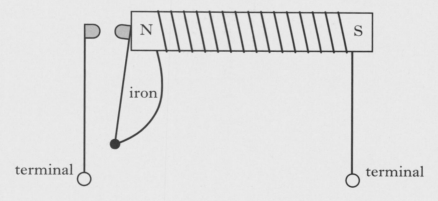

Explain how the circuit breaker operates when the current becomes too high.

....

....

.... 2

Marks | K&U | PS

4. **(continued)**

(b) A 5 ampere circuit breaker is used in a household lighting circuit which has three 60 W lamps as shown below.

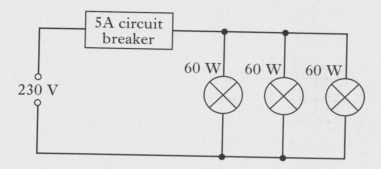

(i) Show that the resistance of **one** lamp is 882 Ω.

Space for working and answer

2

(ii) Calculate the combined resistance of the three lamps in this circuit.

Space for working and answer

2

(iii) Show by calculation whether the circuit breaker will switch off the lamps when all three are lit.

Space for working and answer

3

Marks | K&U | PS

5. A radioactive source is used for medical treatment. The graph shows the activity of this source over a period of time.

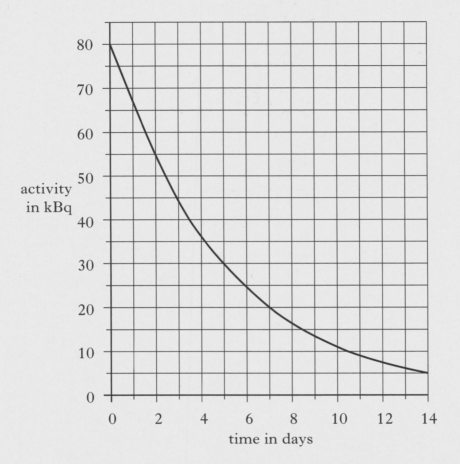

(*a*) Use information from the graph to calculate the half-life of this source.

Space for working and answer

1

5. (continued)

(b) Describe a method that could be used to measure the half-life of this radioactive source, using the apparatus shown. You can ignore background radiation.

clock

stopclock

detector

counter

source

....

....

....

....

....

....

2

(c) A sample of this source is to be given to a patient at 9.30 am on May 17. When the sample is prepared, its initial activity is 200 kBq. The activity of the sample when given to the patient must be 12·5 kBq.

Calculate at what time and on what date the sample should be prepared.

Space for working and answer

2

Marks | K&U | PS

6. The table below gives information about some types of laser.

Type of laser	Wavelength (nm)	Output power (W)
Krypton fluoride	248	1·0
Argon	488	2·0
Helium neon	633	0·005
Rhodamine	570 to 650	50·0
Carbon dioxide	10 600	200·0

(a) The visible spectrum has wavelengths ranging from 400 nm to 700 nm.

   (i) Name one type of laser **from the table** that emits visible radiation.

      1

   (ii) Name one type of laser **from the table** that emits ultraviolet radiation.

      1

   (iii) Give **one** medical use of ultraviolet radiation.

      1

(b) A rhodamine laser can be adjusted to emit a range of wavelengths.

What difference is observed in the light from this laser beam as the wavelength changes?

      ....

      1

(c) The beam from the carbon dioxide laser is used to cut steel. A section of steel is cut in 10 minutes.

Using information from the table, calculate the energy given out by the laser during this cutting process.

Space for working and answer

2

7. A student designs a lie detector using the following circuit.

Moisture detector:

high resistance when dry
low resistance when wet

(a) Name component Q.

.... 1

(b) Suggest a suitable output device that could be used at P to produce an audible output.

.... 1

(c) This lie detector is based on the fact that when a person tells a lie, the moisture on their skin increases. Initially, the person holds the moisture detector in dry hands and component R is adjusted until the output device is silent.

(i) What happens to the resistance of the moisture detector when the person holding it tells a lie?

....

.... 1

(ii) Explain how the circuit operates as a lie detector.

....

....

....

.... 2

[Turn over

Marks | K&U | PS

8. An automatic vending machine accepts 1p, 2p and 5p coins. Four light sensors P, Q, R and S are arranged as shown in the coin slot.

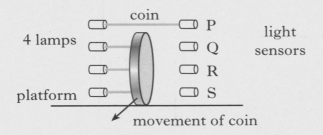

When a coin passes between a lamp and its sensor, the light is blocked. Coins of different diameters block the light from different lamps.

The position of the sensors in relation to the diameters of coins is shown below.

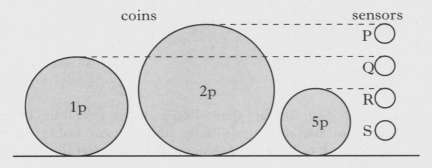

The logic output of the sensors is as follows:

    light blocked   – logic output 1
    light not blocked – logic output 0

(*a*) (i) Name a suitable input device to be used as a sensor.

....   1

    (ii) Complete the truth table for the outputs of the sensors when each of the coins passes between the lamps and the sensors.

	1p coin	*2p coin*	*5p coin*
Sensor P			
Sensor Q			
Sensor R			
Sensor S			

3

K&U | PS

8. **(continued)**

(b) A washer is a metal disc with a hole in the middle. The machine is able to reject washers, when they are inserted instead of coins. A washer the same diameter as a 1p coin blocks the light from reaching sensors Q and S only.

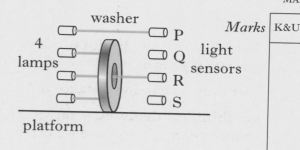

Part of the circuit used is shown below.

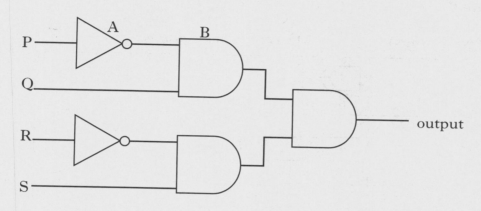

(i) Name gate A.

.... **1**

(ii) Name gate B.

.... **1**

(iii) When a washer is inserted, the logic levels at P, Q, R and S are as shown below.

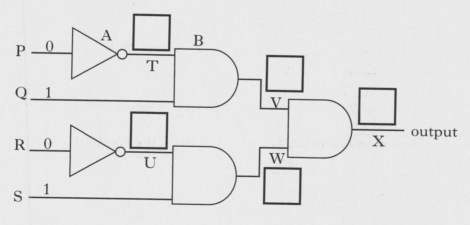

In the boxes on the diagram above, enter the logic levels at each position T, U, V, W and X. **2**

(iv) When a washer is detected, this circuit activates an output device that pushes the washer to reject it.

Name a suitable device to be used as the output device.

.... **1**

Marks   K&U   PS

9. A table from the Highway Code giving overall stopping distances for vehicles is shown.

The overall stopping distance is made up of:

the **thinking distance** – the distance travelled while the driver "thinks" about braking. This distance depends on the driver's reaction time.
plus
the **braking distance** – the distance travelled while braking.

Speed of vehicle (m/s)	Overall stopping distance (m)
8·9	6 6
13·4	9 14
17·8	12 24
26·7	18 55
	thinking distance braking distance

(a) (i) How far does a vehicle travelling at 13·4 m/s travel while the driver thinks about braking?

....   1

(ii) Use information **from the table** to calculate the reaction time.

Space for working and answer

2

9. **(continued)**

(b) A car travels along a road. The driver sees traffic lights ahead change from green and starts to brake as soon as possible. A graph of the car's motion, from the moment the driver sees the traffic lights change, is shown.

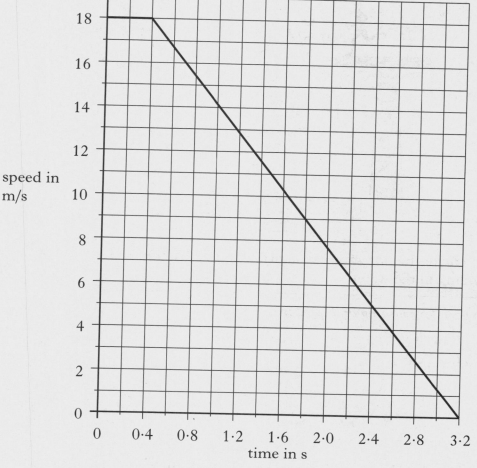

(i) What is **this** driver's reaction time?

....

1

(ii) Calculate the overall stopping distance.

Space for working and answer

3

(iii) Calculate the acceleration of the car from the time the driver applies the brakes.

Space for working and answer

2

10. A student runs along a diving platform and leaves the platform *Marks* horizontally with a speed of 2·0 m/s. The student lands in the water 0·3 s later. Air resistance is negligible.

2·0 m/s

(a) (i) Calculate the horizontal distance travelled by the student before landing in the water.

Space for working and answer

2

(ii) The student has a vertical acceleration of 10 m/s^2.

Calculate the vertical speed as the student enters the water.

Space for working and answer

2

(b) Later the student runs off the end of the same platform with a horizontal speed of 3·0 m/s.

How long does the student take to reach the water this time? Explain your answer.

....

....

....

2

DO NOT WRITE IN THIS MARGIN

Marks | K&U | PS

10. (continued)

(c) The student climbs from the water level to a higher platform. This platform is 5·0 m above the water. The student has a mass of 50 kg.

5·0 m

(i) Calculate the gain in gravitational potential energy of the student.

Space for working and answer

2

(ii) The student drops from the edge of the platform and lands in the water.

Calculate the vertical speed as the student enters the water.

Space for working and answer

2

[Turn over

11. A wind generator on a yacht is used to charge a battery at 12 V.

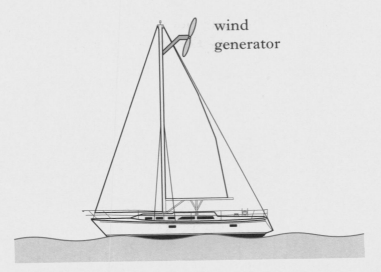

wind
generator

The graph shows the charging current at different wind speeds.

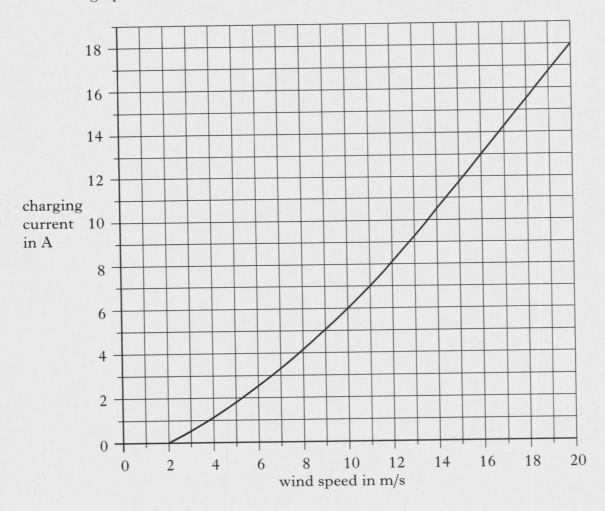

charging
current
in A

wind speed in m/s

(*a*) The wind blows at a speed of 10 m/s.

(i) What is the charging current at this wind speed?

....

1

Marks | K&U | PS

11. **(a)** **(continued)**

(ii) Calculate the electrical power produced by the generator at this wind speed.

Space for working and answer

2

(iii) The wind speed does not change.

Calculate the energy supplied to the battery in 3·5 hours.

Space for working and answer

2

(b) The yacht has a stand-by petrol powered generator to charge the battery.

Why is the petrol generator necessary, in addition to the wind generator?

....

....

1

[Turn over

Marks K&U PS

12. A mains operated air heater contains a fan, driven by a motor, and a heating element. Cold air is drawn into the heater by the fan. The air is heated as it passes the heating element.

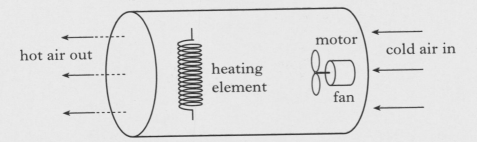

The circuit diagram for the air heater is shown.

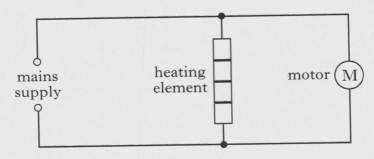

(a) (i) What is the voltage across the heating element when the heater is operating?

.... 1

(ii) What type of circuit is used for the air heater?

.... 1

(b) The following data relates to the heater when the fan rotates at a particular speed.

mass of air passing through per second   0·2 kg
energy supplied to air per second   2000 J
specific heat capacity of air   1000 J/kg °C

(i) Calculate the increase in air temperature.

Space for working and answer

2

Marks | K&U | PS

12. (*b*) **(continued)**

(ii) The motor is adjusted to rotate the fan at a higher speed. This draws a greater mass of air per second through the heater. Explain any difference this causes to the temperature of the hot air.

....

....

....   2

[Turn over

Marks | K&U | PS

13. Titan is the largest of Saturn's moons. The gravitational field strength on Titan is 1·35 N/kg.

(*a*) (i) What is a moon?

....

.... **1**

(ii) What is meant by gravitational field strength?

....

.... **1**

(*b*) Early in 2005, a probe was released from a spacecraft orbiting Titan. The probe, of mass 318 kg, travelled through the atmosphere of Titan.

(i) Calculate the weight of the probe on Titan.

Space for working and answer

2

(ii) As the probe descended through the atmosphere, a parachute attached to it opened.

State why the parachute was used.

....

....

.... **1**

Marks | K&U | PS

13. **(b)** **(continued)**

(iii) The probe carried equipment to analyse the spectral lines of radiation from gases in the atmosphere of Titan. These lines are shown. The spectral lines of a number of elements are also shown.

Spectral lines from gases in Titan's atmosphere

Helium

Hydrogen

Mercury

Nitrogen

Use the spectral lines of the elements to identify which elements are present in the atmosphere of Titan.

....

....

.... 2

[END OF QUESTION PAPER]

YOU MAY USE THE SPACE ON THIS PAGE TO REWRITE ANY ANSWER YOU HAVE DECIDED TO CHANGE IN THE MAIN PART OF THE ANSWER BOOKLET. TAKE CARE TO WRITE IN CAREFULLY THE APPROPRIATE QUESTION NUMBER.

[BLANK PAGE]

C

FOR OFFICIAL USE

K & U   PS

Total Marks

3220/402

NATIONAL
QUALIFICATIONS
2007

WEDNESDAY, 16 MAY
10.50 AM – 12.35 PM

PHYSICS
STANDARD GRADE
Credit Level

Fill in these boxes and read what is printed below.

Full name of centre

Town

Forename(s)

Surname

Date of birth
Day   Month   Year

Scottish candidate number

Number of seat

Reference may be made to the Physics Data Booklet.

1 All questions should be answered.

2 The questions may be answered in any order but all answers must be written clearly and legibly in this book.

3 Write your answer where indicated by the question or in the space provided after the question.

4 If you change your mind about your answer you may score it out and rewrite it in the space provided at the end of the answer book.

5 Before leaving the examination room you must give this book to the invigilator. If you do not, you may lose all the marks for this paper.

6 Any necessary data will be found in the **data sheet** on page two.

7 Care should be taken to give an appropriate number of significant figures in the final answers to questions.

SCOTTISH
QUALIFICATIONS
AUTHORITY

©

DATA SHEET

Speed of light in materials

Material	Speed in m/s
Air	3.0×10^8
Carbon dioxide	3.0×10^8
Diamond	1.2×10^8
Glass	2.0×10^8
Glycerol	2.1×10^8
Water	2.3×10^8

Speed of sound in materials

Material	Speed in m/s
Aluminium	5200
Air	340
Bone	4100
Carbon dioxide	270
Glycerol	1900
Muscle	1600
Steel	5200
Tissue	1500
Water	1500

Gravitational field strengths

	Gravitational field strength on the surface in N/kg
Earth	10
Jupiter	26
Mars	4
Mercury	4
Moon	1.6
Neptune	12
Saturn	11
Sun	270
Venus	9

Specific heat capacity of materials

Material	Specific heat capacity in J/kg °C
Alcohol	2350
Aluminium	902
Copper	386
Diamond	530
Glass	500
Glycerol	2400
Ice	2100
Lead	128
Water	4180

Specific latent heat of fusion of materials

Material	Specific latent heat of fusion in J/kg
Alcohol	0.99×10^5
Aluminium	3.95×10^5
Carbon dioxide	1.80×10^5
Copper	2.05×10^5
Glycerol	1.81×10^5
Lead	0.25×10^5
Water	3.34×10^5

Melting and boiling points of materials

Material	Melting point in °C	Boiling point in °C
Alcohol	−98	65
Aluminium	660	2470
Copper	1077	2567
Glycerol	18	290
Lead	328	1737
Turpentine	−10	156

Specific latent heat of vaporisation of materials

Material	Specific latent heat of vaporisation in J/kg
Alcohol	11.2×10^5
Carbon dioxide	3.77×10^5
Glycerol	8.30×10^5
Turpentine	2.90×10^5
Water	22.6×10^5

SI Prefixes and Multiplication Factors

Prefix	Symbol	Factor	
giga	G	1 000 000 000	$= 10^9$
mega	M	1 000 000	$= 10^6$
kilo	k	1000	$= 10^3$
milli	m	0.001	$= 10^{-3}$
micro	μ	0.000 001	$= 10^{-6}$
nano	n	0.000 000 001	$= 10^{-9}$

Marks | K&U | PS

1. A pupil is sent exam results by a text message on a mobile phone. The frequency of the signal received by the phone is 1900 MHz.

The mobile phone receives radio waves (signals).

(a) What is the speed of radio waves?

$3 \times 10^8 M/S$ ✓

1

(b) Calculate the wavelength of the signal.

Space for working and answer

$\lambda = V/t$ ✗

✓

2

(c) The pupil sends a video message from the mobile phone. The message is transmitted by microwaves. The message travels a total distance of 72 000 km.

Calculate the time between the message being transmitted and received.

Space for working and answer

 $S = \dfrac{D}{T}$ $T = 2.4 \times 10^{-4}$

$T = \dfrac{D}{S}$ ✗

2

2. Radio waves have a wide range of frequencies.

The table gives information about different wavebands.

Waveband	Frequency Range	Example
Low frequency (LF)	30 kHz – 300 kHz	Radio 4
Medium frequency (MF)	300 kHz – 3 MHz	Radio Scotland
High frequency (HF)	3 MHz – 30 MHz	Amateur radio
Very high frequency (VHF)	30 MHz – 300 MHz	Radio 1 FM
Ultra high frequency (UHF)	300 MHz – 3 GHz	BBC 1 and ITV
Super high frequency (SHF)	3 GHz – 30 GHz	Satellite TV

(a) Coastguards use signals of frequency 500 kHz.

What waveband do these signals belong to?

.... M F .... ✓ 1

2. (continued)

(b) The diagram shows how radio signals of different wavelengths are sent between a transmitter and a receiver.

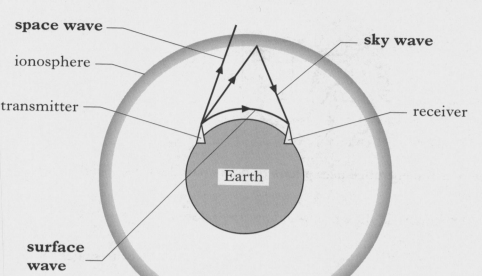

Not to scale

(i) Which of the waves in the diagram shows diffraction?

.... Sky wave ✗ ....

1

(ii) What does this indicate about the wavelength of the diffracted wave compared to the other two waves? ✗

.... ITS higher Than Surfac but lower Than Sky ....

1

(iii) The Earth's ionosphere is shown on the diagram. The ionosphere is a layer of charged particles in the upper atmosphere. High frequency waves are transmitted as sky waves.

Explain how the transmitted waves reach the receiver.

.... ✗ ....

1

(iv) Super high frequency (SHF) signals are shown as space waves on the diagram. Although they can only travel in straight lines, they can be used for communications on Earth between a transmitter and receiver.

Describe how the SHF signals get to the receiver.

.... They Reflec off a Sattelite ✓ ....

....

....

2

3. A door entry system in an office block allows video and audio information to be sent between two people.

(a) A camera at the entrance uses a lens to focus parallel rays of light onto a detector.

Part of the camera is shown in the diagram below.

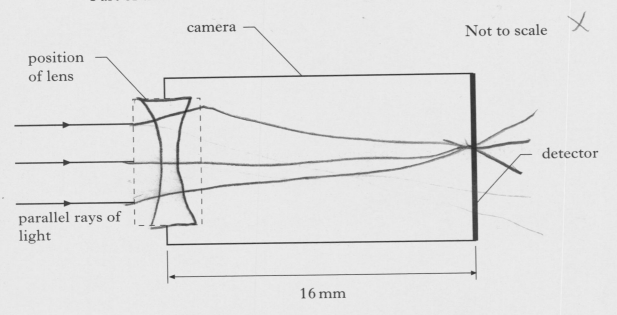

camera

Not to scale

position
of lens

parallel rays of
light

detector

16 mm

(i) Complete the diagram above by:

(A) drawing the lens used;

(B) completing the path of the light rays.

2

(ii) Using information from the diagram, calculate the power of the lens used in the camera.

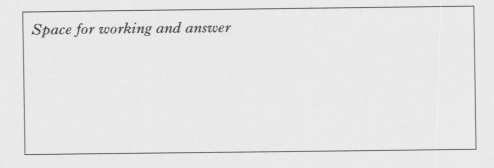

Space for working and answer

2

Marks | K&U | PS

3. **(continued)**

(b) The door entry system uses a black and white television screen.

Describe how a moving picture is seen on the television screen.

Your description must include the terms:

line build up   image retention   brightness variation.

The electrons shoot at
The screen making the line
build up. The Image retention 25
tems per second. The amount of
electrons hitting g screen controls
brightness variation

3

[Turn over

DO NOT
WRITE IN
THIS
MARGIN

Marks | K&U | PS

4. The consumer unit in a house contains a mains switch and circuit breakers for different circuits.

	cooker		shower	water heater	
	A	**B**	**C**	**D**	**E**
mains switch	45 A	30 A	20 A	15 A	5 A

(a) (i) What is the purpose of the mains switch?   circuits✗

To Turn of all mains 1

(ii) Two of the circuits have not been labelled.

Which circuit is: the ring circuit? ...5A........... B

the lighting circuit? .30.A........... E   1

(iii) The current ratings for the ring circuit and the lighting circuit are different.

State another difference between the ring circuit and the lighting circuit.   ✗

The lighting cicuit controlls lights........... 1

DO NOT WRITE IN THIS MARGIN

Marks | K&U | PS

4. (continued)

(*b*) (i) A 25 W lamp is designed to be used with mains voltage.

Calculate the resistance of the lamp.

Space for working and answer

3

(ii) Four of these lamps are connected in parallel.

Calculate the **total** resistance of the lamps.

Space for working and answer

2

[Turn over

DO NOT
WRITE IN
THIS
MARGIN

Marks | K&U | PS

5. Two groups of pupils are investigating the electrical properties of a lamp.

(*a*) Group 1 is given the following equipment:

ammeter; voltmeter; 12 V d.c. supply; lamp; connecting leads.

Complete the circuit diagram to show how this equipment is used to measure the current through, and the voltage across, the lamp.

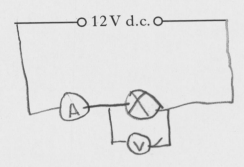

3

(*b*) Group 2 uses the same lamp and is only given the following equipment:

lamp; ohmmeter; connecting leads.

What property of the lamp is measured by the ohmmeter?

...... Resistance 1

(*c*) The results of both groups are combined and recorded in the table below.

I(A)	V(V)	R(Ω)	IV	I^2R
2	12	6	24	24

(i) Use these results to complete the last two columns of the table.

> *Space for working*
> I^2R
> $I \times V =$ $2^2 \times 6 = 24$
> $2 \times 12 = 24$

2

(ii) What quantity is represented by the last two columns of the table?

...... Power 1

(iii) What is the unit for this quantity?

...... W 1

Marks | K&U | PS

6. The thyroid gland, located in the neck, is essential for maintaining good health.

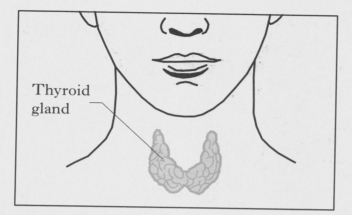

Thyroid gland

(*a*) (i) A radioactive source, which is a gamma radiation emitter, is used as a radioactive tracer for the diagnosis of thyroid gland disorders.

A small quantity of this tracer, with an activity of 20 MBq, is injected into a patient's body. After 52 hours, the activity of the tracer is measured at 1·25 MBq.

Calculate the half life of the tracer.

Space for working and answer

20 ÷ 2 = 10
10 ÷ 2 = 5
5 ÷ 2 = 2.5
2.5 ÷ 2 = 1.25

20 − 1.25
52 ÷ 4 = 13
13 hours

2

(ii) Another radioactive source is used to **treat** cancer of the thyroid gland. This source emits only beta radiation.

Why is this source unsuitable as a **tracer**?

gamma goel Trough The body

1

(iii) The equivalent dose is much higher for the beta emitter than for the gamma emitter.

Why is this higher dose necessary?

1

(*b*) What are the units of equivalent dose?

1

Page eleven

[Turn over

Marks | K&U | PS

7. A newborn baby is given a hearing test. A small device, containing a loudspeaker and a microphone, is placed in the baby's ear.

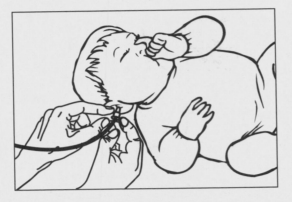

(a) A pulse of audible sound lasting 10 μs is transmitted through the loudspeaker. The sound is played at a level of 80 dB.

(i) Give a reason why this pulse of sound does not cause damage to the baby's hearing.

10 μs is short toime

1

DO NOT
WRITE IN
THIS
MARGIN

7. **(a)** **(continued)**

(ii) The transmitted pulse of sound makes the inner ear vibrate to produce a new sound, which is received by the microphone.

Signals from the transmitted and received sounds are viewed on an oscilloscope screen, as shown below.

The average speed of sound inside the ear is 1500 m/s.

Calculate the distance between the device and the inner ear.

> Space for working and answer

Marks **3**

(iii) Suggest a frequency that could be used for the hearing test.

....

1

(b) An ultrasound scan can be used to produce an image of an unborn baby. Explain how the image of an unborn baby is formed by ultrasound.

.... The ultra Sound bounces Off ....

.... body

....

2

Marks K&U PS

8. A high intensity LED is used as a garden light. The light turns on automatically when it becomes dark.

The light also contains a solar cell which charges a rechargeable battery during daylight hours.

(a) Part of the circuit is shown below.

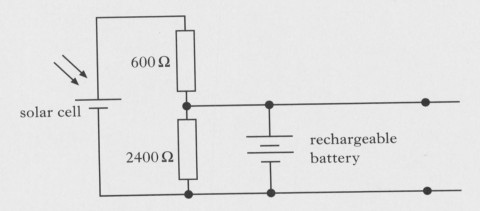

(i) State the energy transformation in a solar cell.

...... light — electricly 1

(ii) At a particular light level, the voltage generated by the solar cell is 1·5 V.

Calculate the voltage across the rechargeable battery at this light level.

Space for working and answer

2

8. (continued)

(b) The LED is switched on using the following circuit.

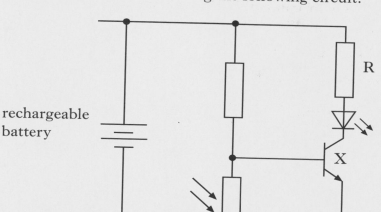

rechargeable
battery

(i) Name component X.

.... Tran Ducer **1**

The graph below shows the voltage across the LDR in this circuit for different light levels.

Light level is measured in lux.

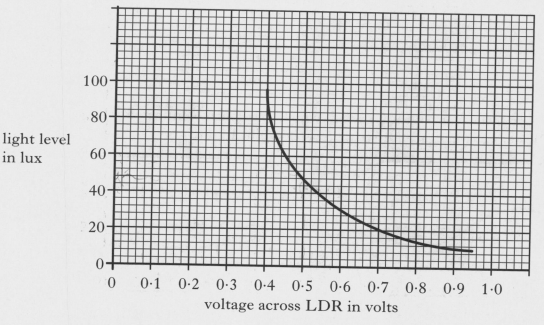

light level
in lux

voltage across LDR in volts

(ii) For the LED to be lit, the voltage across the LDR must be at least 0·7 V.

What is the maximum light level for the LED to be lit?

.... 50 .... **1**

(iii) Explain the purpose of resistor R.

...... ProTuT from back emt **1**

Marks | K&U | PS

9. An electronic tuner for a guitar contains a microphone and an amplifier. The output voltage from the amplifier is 9 V.

(a) The voltage gain of the amplifier is 150.

Calculate the input voltage to the amplifier.

Space for working and answer

2

(b) The tuner is used to measure the frequency of six guitar strings.

The number and frequency of each string is given in the table below.

Number of string	Frequency (Hz)
1	330·0
2	247·0
3	196·0
4	147·0
5	110·0
6	82·5

The tuner has an output socket which has been connected to an oscilloscope. The trace for string 5 is shown in Figure 1.

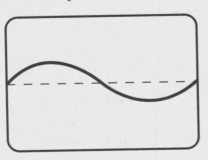

Figure 1

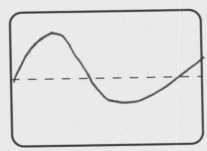

Figure 2

(i) The controls of the oscilloscope are **not** altered.

In Figure 2, draw the trace obtained if string 1 is played **louder** than string 5.

2

(ii) String 3 is plucked.

What is the frequency of the output signal from the amplifier?

1

K&U | PS

10. Cameras placed at 5 km intervals along a stretch of road are used to record the average speed of a car.

The car is travelling on a road which has a speed limit of 100 km/h. The car travels a distance of 5 km in 2·5 minutes.

(*a*) Does the average speed of the car stay within the speed limit?

You must justify your answer with a calculation.

Space for working and answer

$$S = \frac{D}{T}$$

$$S = \frac{5000}{2.5}$$

$$S = 2 kmh$$

Yes

3

(*b*) At one point in the journey, the car speedometer records 90 km/h.

Explain why the average speed for the entire journey is not always the same as the speed recorded on the car speedometer.

....

....

....

....

2

[Turn over

Marks | K&U | PS

11. An aeroplane on an aircraft carrier must reach a minimum speed of 70 m/s to safely take off. The mass of the aeroplane is 28 000 kg.

(a) The aeroplane accelerates from rest to its minimum take off speed in 2 s.

(i) Calculate the acceleration of the aeroplane.

Space for working and answer

$a = \dfrac{V-u}{T}$ $a = 35\,m/s/s$

$a = \dfrac{70}{2}$

2

(ii) Calculate the force required to produce this acceleration.

Space for working and answer

$f = ma$ 980000 N

$f = 28000 \times 35$

2

(iii) The aeroplane's engines provide a total thrust of 240 kN. An additional force is supplied by a catapult to produce the acceleration required.

Calculate the force supplied by the catapult.

Space for working and answer

1

11. (continued)

(b) Later, the same aeroplane travelling at a speed of 65 m/s, touches down on the carrier.

(i) Calculate the kinetic energy of the aeroplane at this speed.

Space for working and answer

2

(ii) The graph shows the motion of the aeroplane from the point when it touches down on the carrier until it stops.

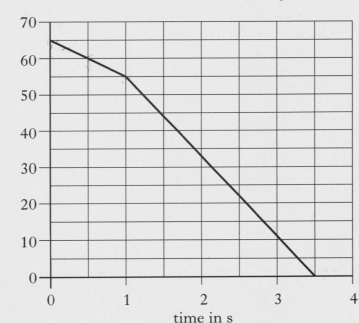

speed in m/s

time in s

Calculate the distance travelled by the aeroplane on the carrier.

Space for working and answer

$S = \frac{D}{T}$

$D = S \times T$

$D = 10 \times 1$

$D = 10$

$\begin{array}{r} 55 \\ \times\ 3.5 \\ \hline 192.5 \end{array}$

2

12. The advertisement below is for a new torch.

Kinetic Torch
No batteries needed – magnet powered!
Bright white LED won't burn out!
30-40 seconds of gentle shaking produces 10-15 minutes of light!
Capacitor holds the charge generated by passing the magnet through the coil.

springs

magnet

coil

LED   movement of magnet

(a) (i) Explain how a voltage is induced in the coil.

The magnetic teild makes votage

2

(ii) What is the effect of shaking the torch faster?

brighter light

1

(iii) Draw the circuit symbol for a capacitor.

Space for symbol

1

(b) When lit, the current in the LED is 20 mA .

Calculate how much charge flows through the LED in 12 minutes.

Space for working and answer

2

Marks | K&U | PS

12. **(continued)**

(c) The torch produces a beam of light.

The diagram shows the LED positioned at the focus of the torch reflector.

LED

reflector

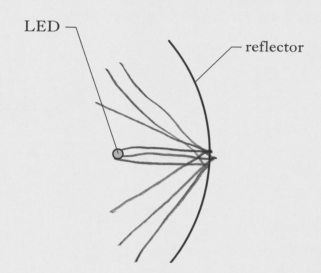

Complete the diagram by drawing light rays to show how the beam of light is produced.

2

[Turn over

Marks | K&U | PS

13. An electric kettle is used to heat 0·4 kg of water.

(a) The initial temperature of the water is 15 °C.

Calculate how much heat energy is required to bring this water to its boiling point of 100 °C.

Space for working and answer

3

(b) The automatic switch on the kettle is not working. The kettle is switched off 5 minutes after it had been switched on.

The power rating of the kettle is 2000 W.

(i) Calculate how much electrical energy is converted into heat energy in this time.

Space for working and answer

2

(ii) Calculate the mass of water changed into steam in this time.

Space for working and answer

3

14. The diagram represents the electromagnetic spectrum in order of increasing wavelength. Some of the radiations have not been named.

Electromagnetic Spectrum

Gamma rays	P	Ultraviolet	Q	Infrared	R	TV and Radio

increasing wavelength →

(a) (i) Name radiation:

P ...... X Ray ......

Q ...... ~~x Ray~~ Visable ......

R ...... fractional   2

(ii) Which radiation in the electromagnetic spectrum has the highest frequency?

....   1

(b) Stars emit **ultraviolet** and **infrared** radiation.

Name a detector for **each** of these two radiations.

Infrared ...... Thermostat ......

Ultraviolet ...... ~~Nongr~~ LDR   2

[Turn over

Marks | K&U | PS

15. In June 2005, a space vehicle called Mars Lander was sent to the planet Mars.

(a) The graph shows the gravitational field strength at different heights above the surface of Mars.

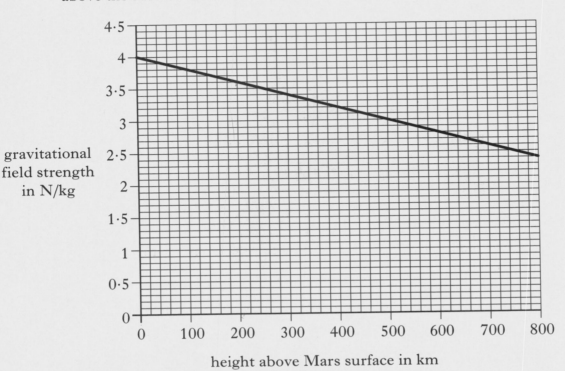

gravitational field strength in N/kg

height above Mars surface in km

(i) The Mars Lander orbited Mars at a height of 200 km above the planet's surface.

What is the value of the gravitational field strength at this height?

.... 3.6 .... **1**

(ii) The Mars Lander, of mass 530 kg, then landed.

Calculate the weight of the Mars Lander on the surface.

Space for working and answer

3

15. (continued)

(b) The Mars Lander released a rover exploration vehicle on to the surface of Mars.

To collect data from the bottom of a large crater, the rover launched a probe horizontally at 30 m/s. The probe took 6 s to reach the bottom of the crater.

(i) Calculate the horizontal distance travelled by the probe.

Space for working and answer

2

(ii) Calculate the vertical speed of the probe as it reached the bottom of the crater.

Space for working and answer

2

[END OF QUESTION PAPER]

YOU MAY USE THE SPACE ON THIS PAGE TO REWRITE ANY ANSWER YOU HAVE DECIDED TO CHANGE IN THE MAIN PART OF THE ANSWER BOOKLET. TAKE CARE TO WRITE IN CAREFULLY THE APPROPRIATE QUESTION NUMBER.

[BLANK PAGE]

C

FOR OFFICIAL USE

K & U	PS

Total Marks

3220/402

NATIONAL
QUALIFICATIONS
2008

FRIDAY, 23 MAY
10.50 AM – 12.35 PM

PHYSICS
STANDARD GRADE
Credit Level

Fill in these boxes and read what is printed below.

Full name of centre

Town

Forename(s)

Surname

Date of birth
Day Month Year   Scottish candidate number   Number of seat

Reference may be made to the Physics Data Booklet.

1 All questions should be answered.

2 The questions may be answered in any order but all answers must be written clearly and legibly in this book.

3 Write your answer where indicated by the question or in the space provided after the question.

4 If you change your mind about your answer you may score it out and rewrite it in the space provided at the end of the answer book.

5 Before leaving the examination room you must give this book to the invigilator. If you do not, you may lose all the marks for this paper.

6 Any necessary data will be found in the **data sheet** on page three.

7 Care should be taken to give an appropriate number of significant figures in the final answers to questions.

[BLANK PAGE]

DATA SHEET

Speed of light in materials

Material	Speed in m/s
Air	$3 \cdot 0 \times 10^8$
Carbon dioxide	$3 \cdot 0 \times 10^8$
Diamond	$1 \cdot 2 \times 10^8$
Glass	$2 \cdot 0 \times 10^8$
Glycerol	$2 \cdot 1 \times 10^8$
Water	$2 \cdot 3 \times 10^8$

Speed of sound in materials

Material	Speed in m/s
Aluminium	5200
Air	340
Bone	4100
Carbon dioxide	270
Glycerol	1900
Muscle	1600
Steel	5200
Tissue	1500
Water	1500

Gravitational field strengths

	Gravitational field strength on the surface in N/kg
Earth	10
Jupiter	26
Mars	4
Mercury	4
Moon	1·6
Neptune	12
Saturn	11
Sun	270
Venus	9

Specific heat capacity of materials

Material	Specific heat capacity in J/kg °C
Alcohol	2350
Aluminium	902
Copper	386
Glass	500
Glycerol	2400
Ice	2100
Lead	128
Silica	1033
Water	4180

Specific latent heat of fusion of materials

Material	Specific latent heat of fusion in J/kg
Alcohol	$0 \cdot 99 \times 10^5$
Aluminium	$3 \cdot 95 \times 10^5$
Carbon dioxide	$1 \cdot 80 \times 10^5$
Copper	$2 \cdot 05 \times 10^5$
Glycerol	$1 \cdot 81 \times 10^5$
Lead	$0 \cdot 25 \times 10^5$
Water	$3 \cdot 34 \times 10^5$

Melting and boiling points of materials

Material	Melting point in °C	Boiling point in °C
Alcohol	−98	65
Aluminium	660	2470
Copper	1077	2567
Glycerol	18	290
Lead	328	1737
Turpentine	−10	156

Specific latent heat of vaporisation of materials

Material	Specific latent heat of vaporisation in J/kg
Alcohol	$11 \cdot 2 \times 10^5$
Carbon dioxide	$3 \cdot 77 \times 10^5$
Glycerol	$8 \cdot 30 \times 10^5$
Turpentine	$2 \cdot 90 \times 10^5$
Water	$22 \cdot 6 \times 10^5$

SI Prefixes and Multiplication Factors

Prefix	Symbol	Factor	
giga	G	1 000 000 000	$= 10^9$
mega	M	1 000 000	$= 10^6$
kilo	k	1000	$= 10^3$
milli	m	0·001	$= 10^{-3}$
micro	μ	0·000 001	$= 10^{-6}$
nano	n	0·000 000 001	$= 10^{-9}$

Marks

1. A high definition television picture has 1080 lines and there are 25 pictures produced each second.

(*a*)   (i)   Calculate how long it takes to produce one picture on the screen.

> *Space for working and answer*

1

(ii) Explain why a continuous moving picture is seen on the television screen and not 25 individual pictures each second.

....

....

....   2

(*b*) The television picture is in colour.

(i)   Which **two** colours are used to produce magenta on the screen?

....   1

(ii) Due to a fault, the colour yellow appears as orange on the screen. Which colour should be reduced in brightness to correct this problem?

....   1

DO NOT
WRITE IN
THIS
MARGIN

K&U | PS

Marks

2. A television company is making a programme in China.

    Britain receives television pictures live from China. The television signals are transmitted using microwaves. The microwave signals travel from China **via** a satellite, which is in a geostationary orbit.

    (*a*) State what is meant by a geostationary orbit.

    .... **1**

    (*b*) The diagram shows the position of the transmitter and receiver. Complete the diagram to show the path of the microwave signals **from** China **to** Britain.

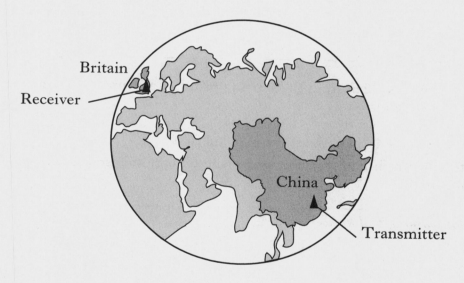

    2

    (*c*) The frequency of the microwave signals being used for transmission is 8 GHz.

    (i) What is the speed of the microwaves?

    .... **1**

    (ii) Calculate the wavelength of these microwaves.

    ```
    Space for working and answer
    ```

    2

Marks

3. In a sprint race at a school sports day, the runners start when they hear the sound of the starting pistol. An electronic timer is also started when the pistol is fired into the air.

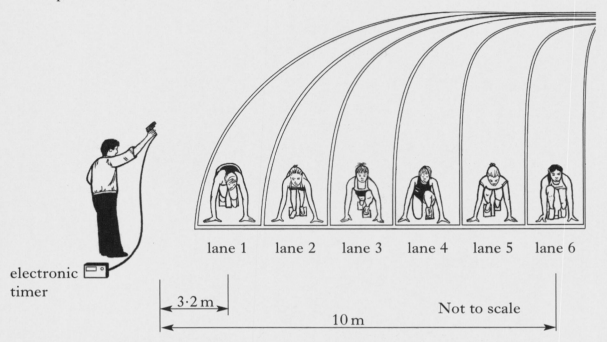

lane 1   lane 2   lane 3   lane 4   lane 5   lane 6

electronic timer

3·2 m

10 m

Not to scale

The runner in lane 1 is 3·2 m from the starting pistol. The runner in lane 6 is 10 m from the starting pistol.

(a) The runner in lane 1 hears the starting pistol first.

Calculate how much later the runner in lane 6 hears this sound after the runner in lane 1.

Space for working and answer

3

DO NOT
WRITE IN
THIS
MARGIN

K&U   PS

Marks

3. (continued)

(b) A sensor detects each runner crossing the finishing line to record their time.

The table gives information about the race.

Place	Lane	Time (s)
1st	1	13·11
2nd	6	13·12
3rd	3	13·21

Using your answer to part (a), explain why the runner in lane 6 should have been awarded first place.

> *Space for working and answer*

2

(c) One runner of mass 60 kg has a speed of 9 m/s when crossing the finishing line.

Calculate the kinetic energy of the runner at this point.

> *Space for working and answer*

2

[Turn over

Marks

4. A student has four resistors labelled A, B, C and D. The student sets up Circuit 1 to identify the value of each resistor.

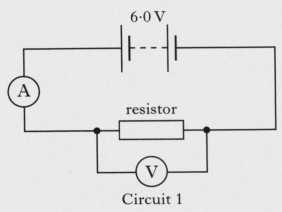

6·0 V

resistor

Circuit 1

Each resistor is placed in the circuit in turn and the following results are obtained.

Resistor	Voltage across resistor (V)	Current (A)
A	6·0	0·017
B	6·0	0·027
C	6·0	0·050
D	6·0	0·033

(a) (i) Show, **by calculation**, which of the resistors has a value of 120 Ω.

Space for working and answer

3

Marks

4. (a) (continued)

(ii) The student then sets up Circuit 2 to measure the resistance of each
resistor.

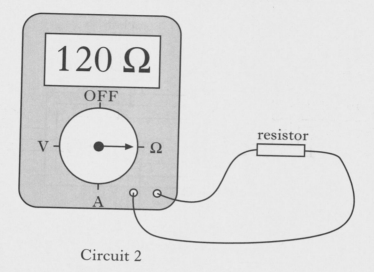

Circuit 2

State **one** advantage of using Circuit 2 to measure the resistance
compared to using Circuit 1.

....

1

(b) The resistances of the other three resistors are 180 Ω, 220 Ω and 360 Ω.
The student connects all four resistors in series.
Calculate the total resistance.

Space for working and answer

2

[Turn over

Marks

5. The diagram shows three household circuits connected to a consumer unit.

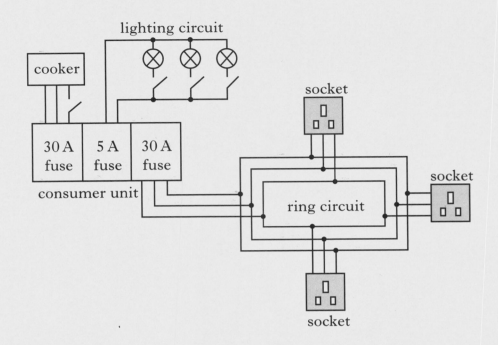

(*a*) (i) State **one** advantage of a ring circuit.

.... **1**

(ii) State the value of mains voltage.

.... **1**

(*b*) Each of the lamps in the lighting circuit has a power rating of 100 W. One of the lamps is switched on.

(i) Calculate the current in the lamp.

Space for working and answer

2

DO NOT WRITE IN THIS MARGIN

K&U	PS

Marks

5. (*b*) (continued)

(ii) Explain why a house with twenty 100 W lamps requires two separate lighting circuits.

....

.... **2**

[Turn over

Marks

6. A short-sighted person has difficulty seeing the picture on a cinema screen.

   Figure 1 shows rays of light from the screen entering an eye of the person until the rays reach the retina.

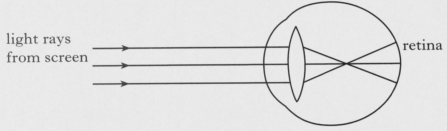

Figure 1

(a) (i) In the dotted box in Figure 2, draw the shape of lens that would correct this eye defect.

1

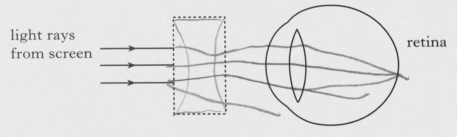

Figure 2

(ii) In Figure 2, complete the path of the rays of light from this lens until they reach the retina.

2

Marks

6. (continued)

(b) Doctors can use an endoscope to examine internal organs of a patient. The endoscope has two separate bundles of optical fibres that are flexible.

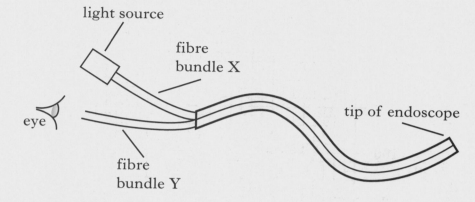

A section of optical fibre used in the endoscope is shown below.

(i) Complete the diagram to show how light is transmitted along the optical fibre.

2

(ii) Explain the purpose of each bundle of optical fibres in the endoscope.

Fibre bundle X ....

....

Fibre bundle Y ....

.... **2**

(iii) The tip of the endoscope that is inside the patient is designed to be very flexible. Suggest **one** reason for this.

.... **1**

[Turn over

DO NOT
WRITE I
THIS
MARGII

K&U   P$

Marks

7. A hospital technician is working with a radioactive source. The graph shows the activity of the source over a period of time.

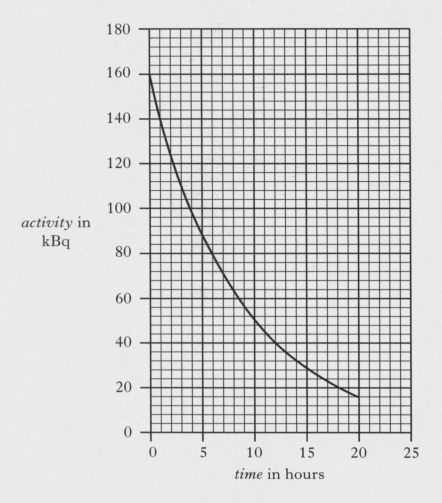

(a)   (i)   State what is meant by the term *half-life*.

.... 1

(ii) Use information from the graph to calculate the half-life of the radioactive source.

Space for working and answer

1

Marks

7. (a) (continued)

(iii) The initial activity of the source is 160 kBq.

Calculate the activity, in kBq, of the radioactive source after four half-lives.

Space for working and answer

1

(b) As a safety precaution the technician wears a film badge when working with radioactive sources. The film badge contains photographic film. Light cannot enter the badge.

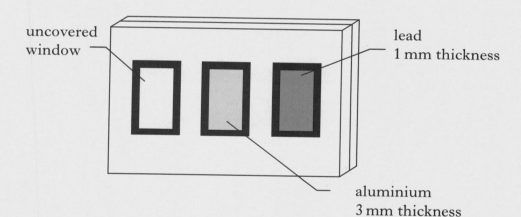

uncovered window

lead 1 mm thickness

aluminium 3 mm thickness

Describe how the film badge indicates the **type** and **amount** of radiation received.

....

....

....

.... 2

[Turn over

DO NOT
WRITE IN
THIS
MARGIN

K&U | PS

Marks

8. A torch contains five identical LEDs connected to a 3·0 V battery as shown.

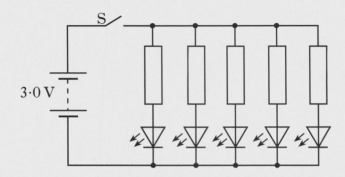

(*a*) State the purpose of the resistor connected in series with each LED.

.... 1

(*b*) When lit, each LED operates at a voltage of 1·8 V and a current of 30 mA.

   (i) Calculate the value of the resistor in series with each LED.

         Space for working and answer

          3

   (ii) Calculate the total current from the supply when all five LEDs are lit.

         Space for working and answer

          1

K&U | PS

DO NOT WRITE IN THIS MARGIN

K&U PS

Marks

8. **(*b*) (continued)**

(iii) Calculate the power supplied by the battery when all five LEDs are lit.

Space for working and answer

2

(*c*) State **one** advantage of using five LEDs rather than a single filament lamp in the torch.

.... 1

[Turn over

Marks

9. An electronic device produces a changing light pattern when it detects music, but only when it is in the dark.

The device contains the logic circuit shown.

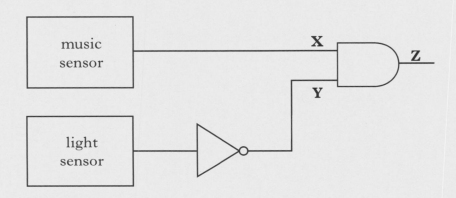

The music sensor produces logic 1 when the music is on and logic 0 when the music is off.

The light sensor produces logic 1 when it detects light and logic 0 when it is dark.

(*a*) (i) Suggest a suitable input device for the light sensor.

....   **1**

(ii) Complete the truth table for the logic levels at points **X**, **Y** and **Z** in the circuit.

Music	Light level	X	Y	Z
off	dark			
off	light			
on	dark			
on	light			

3

Marks

9. (continued)

(b) The device detects music from a CD player. The CD player contains an amplifier that produces an output voltage of 5·6 V when connected to a loudspeaker of resistance 3·2 Ω.

(i) Calculate the output power of the amplifier.

Space for working and answer

2

(ii) The input power to the amplifier is 4·9 mW.

Calculate the power gain of the amplifier.

Space for working and answer

2

(iii) One particular signal from the CD to the amplifier has a frequency of 170 Hz.

What is the frequency of the output signal from the amplifier?

.... 1

[Turn over

DO NOT
WRITE IN
THIS
MARGIN

K&U PS

Marks

10. A railway train travels uphill between two stations.

Information about the train and its journey is given below.

average speed of train	5 m/s
time for journey	150 s
power of train	120 kW
mass of train plus passengers	20 000 kg

(*a*) Calculate the energy used by the train during the journey.

Space for working and answer

2

Marks

10. **(continued)**

(b) Calculate the height gained by the train during the journey.

> *Space for working and answer*

2

(c) Suggest why the actual height gained by the train is less than the value calculated in part (b).

....

.... 1

[Turn over

11. A windsurfer takes part in a race. The windsurfer takes 120 seconds to complete the race. The total mass of the windsurfer and the board is 90 kg.

The graph shows how the speed of the windsurfer and board changes with time during part of the race.

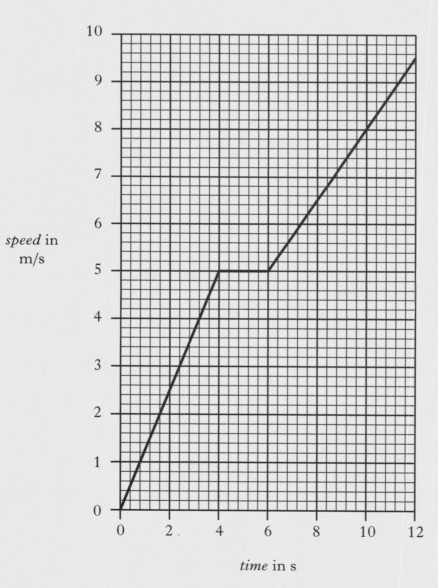

speed in m/s

time in s

11. (continued)

(a) (i) Calculate the acceleration of the windsurfer and board during the first 4 s of the race.

Space for working and answer

2

(ii) Calculate the unbalanced force causing this acceleration.

Space for working and answer

2

(b) Calculate the total distance travelled by the windsurfer during the 12 s time interval shown on the graph.

Space for working and answer

2

(c) What can be said about the horizontal forces acting on the windsurfer between 4 s and 6 s?

....

1

[Turn over

12. An underwater generator is designed to produce electricity from water currents in the sea.

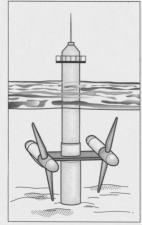

The output power of the generator depends on the speed of the water current as shown in Graph 1.

Graph 1

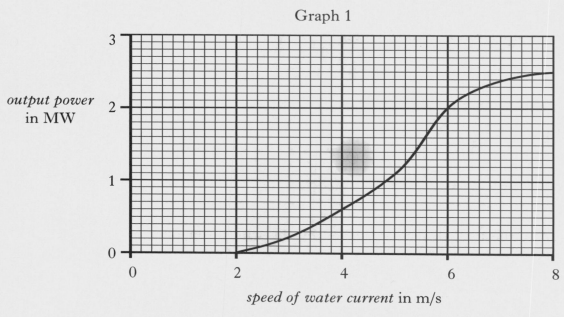

The speed of the water current is recorded at different times of the day shown in Graph 2.

Graph 2

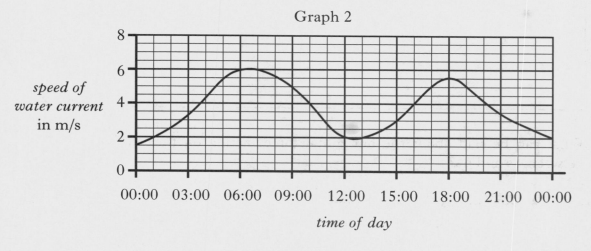

Page twenty-four

12. (continued)

(a) (i) State the output power of the generator at 09:00.

.... 1

(ii) State **one** disadvantage of using this type of generator.

.... 1

(b) The voltage produced by the generator is stepped-up by a transformer.

At one point in the day the electrical current in the primary coils of the transformer is 900 A and the voltage is 2000 V.

The transformer is 96% efficient.

(i) Calculate the output power of the transformer at this time.

```
Space for working and answer
```

3

(ii) State **one** reason why a transformer is not 100% efficient.

.... 1

[Turn over

Marks

12.   (continued)

(*c*) Three different types of electrical generator, X, Y and Z are tested in a special tank with a current of water as shown to find out the efficiency of each generator.

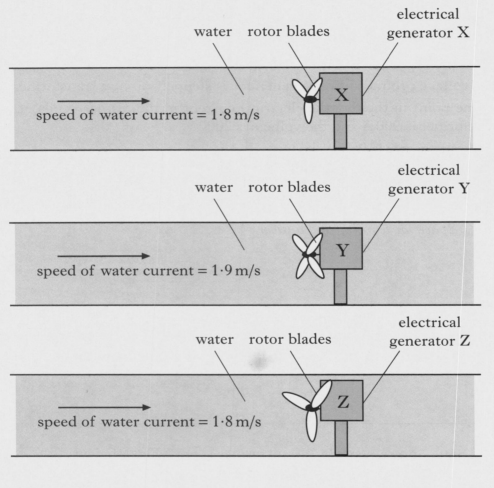

Give **two** reasons why this is not a fair test.

....

....   **1**

DO NOT WRITE IN THIS MARGIN

K&U PS

Marks

13. In the reactor of a nuclear power station, neutrons split uranium nuclei to produce heat in what is known as a "chain reaction".

(a) Explain what is meant by the term "chain reaction".

....

.... **2**

(b) In the nuclear power station, 1 kg of uranium fuel produces 4 200 000 MJ of heat. In a coal-fired power station 1 kg of coal produces 28 MJ of heat. Calculate how many kilograms of coal are required to produce the same amount of heat as 1 kg of uranium.

Space for working and answer

1

(c) A power station uses an a.c. generator to convert kinetic energy from a turbine into electrical energy. A diagram of an a.c. generator is shown.

rotating electromagnetic coils

stator coils

electrical output

(i) Explain how the a.c. generator works.

....

.... **2**

(ii) State **two** changes that can be made to the generator to increase the output power.

Change 1: ....

Change 2: **2**

DO NOT
WRITE I
THIS
MARGIN

K&U   PS

Marks

14. A team of astronomers observes a star 200 light-years away.

(a) State what is meant by the term "light-year".

.... **1**

(b) Images of the star are taken with three different types of telescope as shown.

  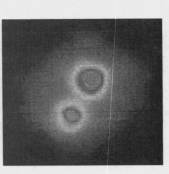

Telescope A   Telescope B   Telescope C
visible light   infrared   X-ray

(i) Explain why different types of telescope are used to detect signals from space.

....

.... **2**

(ii) Place the telescopes in order of the increasing wavelength of the radiation which they detect.

.... **1**

(iii) State a detector that could be used in telescope C.

.... **1**

(c) Telescope A is a refracting telescope with an objective lens of focal length 400 mm and diameter 80 mm.

(i) Calculate the power of the objective lens.

Space for working and answer

2

14. (*c*) **(continued)**

(ii) One of the astronomers suggests replacing the objective lens in this telescope with one of larger diameter.

State an advantage of doing this.

.... 1

[Turn over for Question 15 on *Page thirty*

Marks

15. (*a*) A spacecraft is used to transport astronauts and equipment to a space station. On its return from space the spacecraft must re-enter the Earth's atmosphere. The spacecraft has a heat shield made from special silica tiles to prevent the inside from becoming too hot.

(i) Why does the spacecraft increase in temperature when it re-enters the atmosphere?

.... 1

(ii) The mass of the heat shield is $3 \cdot 5 \times 10^3$ kg and the gain in heat energy of the silica tiles is $4 \cdot 7$ GJ.

Calculate the increase in temperature of the silica tiles.

Space for working and answer

3

(iii) Explain why the actual temperature rise of the silica tiles is less than the value calculated in (*a*)(ii).

....

.... 1

(*b*) When a piece of equipment was loaded on to the spacecraft on Earth, two people were required to lift it.

One person was able to lift the same piece of equipment in the Space Station.

Explain why one person was able to lift the equipment in the Space Station.

.... 1

[END OF QUESTION PAPER]

**YOU MAY USE THE SPACE ON THIS PAGE TO REWRITE ANY ANSWER
YOU HAVE DECIDED TO CHANGE IN THE MAIN PART OF THE ANSWER
BOOKLET. TAKE CARE TO WRITE IN CAREFULLY THE APPROPRIATE
QUESTION NUMBER.**

[BLANK PAGE]

[BLANK PAGE]

[BLANK PAGE]

[BLANK PAGE]

Acknowledgements

Leckie & Leckie is grateful to the copyright holders, as credited, for permission to use their material:

The following companies have very generously given permission to reproduce their copyright material free of charge: Philips International B.V. for a photograph of a Philips electric toothbrush (2005 Credit paper p 22). Philips trademarks are owned by Koninklijke Philips Electronics N.V. who have given permission for their trademarks to be reproduced in this publication.